REMEMBERING

RANDOLPH

COUNTY

REMEMBERING

RANDOLPH

COUNTY

tales from

THE CENTER OF THE TAR HEEL STATE

CHIP WOMICK

Charleston · London
THE
History
PRESS

Published by The History Press
Charleston, SC 29403
www.historypress.net

Images from the Randolph County Public Library can be accessed at:
http://www.randolphlibrary.org/historicalphotos.htm.

First published 2008

Manufactured in the United States

ISBN 978.1.59629.489.9

Library of Congress Cataloging-in-Publication Data

Womick, Chip.
Remembering Randolph County: tales from the center of the Tar Heel State / Chip
Womick.
p. cm.
ISBN 978-1-59629-489-9
1. Randolph County (N.C.)--History--Anecdotes. 2. Randolph County (N.C.)--Biography-
-Anecdotes. 3. Historic sites--North Carolina--Randolph County--Anecdotes. 4. Historic
buildings--North Carolina--Randolph County--Anecdotes. 5. Randolph County (N.C.)--
History, Local--Anecdotes. I. Title.
F262.R2W66 2008
975.6'61--dc22
                                    2008026578

Notice: The information in this book is true and complete to the best of our knowledge. It is offered without guarantee on the part of the author or The History Press. The author and The History Press disclaim all liability in connection with the use of this book.

CONTENTS

THE TRAGIC TALE OF NAOMI WISE

The inscription on Naomi Wise's once-white gravestone tells little:

Naomi Wise
1789–1808

Wise's marble marker, now gray with age, stands in the Providence Friends Meeting cemetery north of Randleman. According to a 1985 book entitled *The Architectural History of Randolph County, N.C.* by Lowell McKay Whatley Jr., the current marker was erected in 1949 to replace the original stone. The first meetinghouse, built when the meeting was founded in 1769, stood next to the graveyard. The current brick meetinghouse stands across the road.

Today, few Randolph County residents know the name Naomi Wise, much less know of her story.

Two centuries ago, the tale of Wise's tragic and untimely demise was trumpeted far and wide, even commemorated in song.

Legend tells us that young Naomi was an orphan who fell in love with a fellow named Jonathan Lewis. North Carolina's oldest-known ballad, "The Ballad of Naomi Wise," recounts how Lewis, who wanted to marry another, drowned Naomi in the Deep River.

The story about the girl's murder and the subsequent arrest of Lewis was passed by word of mouth for most of the nineteenth century. Then, in April 1874, "The Story of Naomi Wise" was published in a newspaper called the *Greensboro Patriot*. A man named Charlie Vernon wrote the account.

A weathered marker for Naomi Wise stands in the Providence Friends Meeting cemetery north of Randleman. *Naomi Wise; Randolph County Historical Photographs; Randolph County Public Library—Randolph Room.*

Sixty years later, in 1944, the Randleman Rotary Club published a booklet that included Vernon's article along with other historical writings. In a foreword, Randleman Rotarians noted that it was believed that the author of the story detailing Naomi's short life and death was Dr. Braxton Craven, using a pen name. Craven was president of Randolph County's Trinity College, which moved to Durham in 1892 and later became Duke University.

The typical prose of 1874 was flowery, extravagant. The sad story of Naomi Wise lent itself well to embellishment.

About ninety years ago, there lived where New Salem now is, in the northern part of Randolph County, North Carolina, a very open and warm hearted gentleman by the name of William Adams. A few families of nature's noblest quality lived in the vicinity. They were not emphatically rich, but were what our people called good livers; they were honest, hospitable and kind; they knew neither the luxuries nor the vices of high life. Their farms supplied enough for their own tables, and surplus sufficient for a brisk trade with Fayetteville.

Young Naomi lived with the Adams family.

She had early been thrown upon the cold charity of the world, and she had received the frozen crumbs of that charity. Her size was medium; her figure beautifully formed; her face handsome and expressive; her eye keen yet mild; her words soft and winning. She was left without father to protect, mother to counsel, brothers and sisters to love, or friends with whom to associate.

Nearby, Vernon writes, lived a family feared in the region. The young Jonathan Lewis was a member of this clan.

This was in every respect a peculiar family, peculiar in appearance, in character, and in destiny. The Lewises were tall, broad, muscular and very powerful men. In the manner of fighting very common at that time, viz: to lay aside all clothing but pantaloons, and then try for victory by striking with the fist, scratching, gouging and biting, a Lewis was not to be vanquished. The family were the lions of the country. This character was eminently pugnacious. Nearly all of them drank to intoxication; aware of power, they insulted whom they listed; they sought occasions of quarrel as a Yankee does gold dust in California. They rode through plantations; killed their neighbors' cattle; took fish from other men's traps; said what they pleased, all more for contention than gain.

Unfortunately for Naomi, she was quite smitten by young Jonathan, as any young lady of the day might have been, according to Vernon.

If he had lived in Scotland he would have been a worthy companion for Sir William Wallace or Robert Bruce; in England, he would have vied with the Black Prince in coolness and bravery; in France he might have stood by the side of McDonald, in the central charge at Wagram; in our own revolution his bravery and power would, perhaps, have saved the day at Brandywine. He was composed of the fiercest elements; his wrath was like whirlwinds and scathing lightning; his smile like sunbeams bursting through a cloud, illumined every countenance upon which it fell.

Which included, of course, the countenance of young Naomi. As fate would have it, Naomi's fair face and figure caught the attention of young Lewis. He wooed the girl, won her heart and she believed that they would wed.

Then his mother stepped in. She wanted her son to marry someone of higher standing. She preferred for her son's attentions to be directed toward Hettie Elliott, the sister of his employer, Asheboro lawyer Benjamin Elliott. Jonathan worked as a clerk for Elliott, who apparently approved of the match.

Alas, poor Naomi stood in the way. The story goes that Jonathan decided to remove her from the picture. He told her that he would come for her on horseback, so they could ride to Asheboro and be married by a magistrate. On the way, however, he drowned her in the Deep River.

When Naomi's body was found, the evidence, though circumstantial, pointed to Lewis. He was arrested, but he broke out of jail and fled. When local authorities later learned that he was living in Kentucky, a party of men traveled there to bring him back to face justice.

His trial took place in neighboring Guilford County in 1815. By that time, the material witnesses had died or moved away. Lewis was acquitted of killing Naomi. He returned to Kentucky, but lived just a few more years.

In the end, Vernon writes, Lewis came clean.

For two days the death rattle had been in his throat, and yet he retained his reason and speech. Finally he bid every person leave the room, but his father, and to him he confessed all the circumstances we have detailed. He declared that while in prison Naomi was ever before him; his sleep was

*broken by her cries for mercy, and in the dim twilight her shadowy form
was ever before him, holding up her imploring hands.*

"The Ballad of Naomi Wise" is included in folk song collections across
the United States. It can be sung to the early American traditional hymn
"How Firm a Foundation," or to any tune with meter 11/11/11/11.

*Come all you good people, I'd have you draw near,
A sorrowful story you quickly shall hear;
A story now I'll tell you about Naomi Wise,
How she was deluded by Lewis' lies.*

*He promised to marry and used me quite well,
But conduct contrary, I sadly must tell;
He promised to meet me at Adams' spring,
He promised me marriage and many fine things.*

*Still nothing he gave but yet flattered the case.
He said we'll be married and have no disgrace;
Come get up behind me, we'll go up to town,
And there we'll be married, in union be bound.*

*I got up behind him and straightway did go
To the banks of Deep River where the water did flow.
He says, "Now Naomi, I'll tell you my mind,
I intend here to drown you and leave you behind."*

*O! Pity your infant and spare me my life,
Let me go rejected and not be your wife;
"No pity, no pity," this monster did cry,
"In Deep River's bottom your body shall lie."*

*The wretch did choke her, as we understand
And threw her in the water below the mill dam.
Be it murder or treason, oh, what a great crime
To murder poor Naomi and leave her behind.*

Naomi was missing, they all did well know
And hunting for her to the river did go;
And there found her floating on the water so deep,
Which caused all the people to sigh and to weep.

The neighbors were sent for to see the great sight,
While she lay floating all that long night.
So early next morning the inquest was held.
The jury correctly the murder did tell.

A GOVERNOR
FROM RANDOLPH

Residents of Asheboro in 1824 might have chuckled, or even laughed aloud, if someone had suggested that a shy newcomer named Jonathan Worth, a fellow who had moved to town to practice law, would one day be their governor.

In the beginning, he struggled to establish a successful practice. At twenty-two, Worth was neither imposing of figure nor impressive in speech. Worth could not much enhance his physical stature, but he chose to improve his oratorical skills using what might be called a sink-or-swim strategy. He entered politics, where the art of public speaking is crucial to earning the support and the votes of both colleagues and constituents. The historical record tells us that Worth never achieved eloquence. He developed instead a forceful and convincing manner of speech that coupled with an exacting and methodical work ethic to serve him well during four decades of public service, including several terms in the state legislature, a time as state treasurer and two terms as governor.

He was the first, and to date the only, Randolph County resident ever to serve as governor.

His time in office, from 1865 to 1868, came on the heels of the Civil War, during the early days of Reconstruction—a time of transition when it would have been difficult for any leader to please widely divergent groups that included his fellow citizens, both those who had favored the war and those who had not, as well as Northern military authorities and the federal administration in Washington, D.C.

Jonathan Worth of Asheboro was governor of North Carolina after the Civil War. *Jonathan Worth; Randolph County Historical Photographs; Randolph County Public Library—Randolph Room.*

By the time he sat at the helm of the Tar Heel State, Worth was a much different man than the diffident attorney who settled in Asheboro forty years earlier. An 1867 article in the Charleston *Chronicle* described him as "a quiet little gentleman sharp as a briar, and with a well of wisdom at the root of every gray hair."

Worth was born in Guilford County, Randolph's neighbor to the north, on November 18, 1802. His parents, Dr. David and Eunice Worth, were Quakers. He attended one of the best schools in the state, Greensboro's Caldwell Institute, before studying law in Orange County under the tutelage of Archibald DeBow Murphey, a judge and state legislator who is sometimes referred to as the "Father of Education" in North Carolina. Later, Worth married Judge Murphey's niece, Martitia Daniel.

When Murphey was a legislator, his proposals to create a publicly financed system of education were ignored. Twenty years later, he saw his protégé take up the cause when Worth, as chairman of a legislative committee on education in 1841, drafted a public school law. (Worth also taught his slaves to read though it was against the law.)

In the years following his election to the House of Commons (the forerunner to the House of Representatives in the General Assembly of North Carolina) in 1830, Worth's law office prospered. He developed other business interests, too, ranging far from the legal profession to include merchandising, textile manufacturing, real estate and shipping. He operated several plantations and a turpentine tract and was a large shareholder in the plank road from Fayetteville to Salem.

Worth opposed the war and stood against secession for a long time. In January 1861, when he was a state senator, he urged his constituents in Randolph and Alamance Counties to vote against a convention of delegates who would contemplate withdrawal from the Union:

> *I can see no way by which it can do any good, and I fear it may do much mischief. Such a convention is a modern invention of South Carolina, to bring about a sort of legalized revolution. It has been adopted in most of the Southern States. All its original advocates were disunionists.*
>
> *Whenever such a convention has assembled, it has asserted the power to sever the State from the Union, and declare it an independent government. Under my oath to support the Constitution of the United States, I could not vote to call a convention to overthrow that instrument.*

When the votes were counted in February of 1861, Unionists carried the day by a margin of fewer than one thousand votes. Little more than a month after the April 12, 1861 bombardment of Fort Sumter near Charleston, South Carolina, however, delegates to a convention voted to join the Confederate States of America.

Worth remained loyal to his state despite his misgivings about the war and, in 1862, was elected by acclamation of the legislature as state treasurer. His financial stewardship proved a boon for the state. While Confederate currency grew weaker as the war progressed, North Carolina's treasury notes did not falter and the state enjoyed a superior credit rating.

He did not buy Confederate bonds during the war, but Worth put his own money into real estate, which he viewed as a more prudent investment given his strong belief that the South was "committing suicide." Even as the war raged in 1864, he was a partner in the purchase of three hundred acres deep in Yankee territory on Long Island, New York.

After the war, Worth continued as provisional treasurer at the request of the provisional governor, William Holden, who was appointed by President Andrew Johnson to replace Governor Zebulon Vance at the war's end. Worth resigned a few months later to run as the nominee of the Conservative Party (a coalition of Democrats and former Whigs) against Holden in a special election. Holden ran on the ticket of the National Union Party.

As governor, Worth supported President Johnson and worked to restore relations between his state and the Union.

Worth refused to run for reelection in 1868; in fact, he did not recognize the election of William Holden as legitimate. When he left office, he wrote to Holden, "I surrender the office to you under what I deem military duress."

The rigors of his post had taken a toll on Worth's health and he died at Sharon (his home in the state capital of Raleigh) in September of 1869, little more than a year after leaving office.

A state historical marker stands by the street in front of the courthouse. It says little: "Jonathan Worth. Governor. 1865–1868. State Treasurer, 1862–1865. Home stood one block south." The monument on Worth's grave in Raleigh's Oakwood Cemetery also says little: "Legislator, chief financial officer and governor of his native state. Faithful in all."

Most residents of twenty-first-century Randolph County probably know little, if anything, about one of the county's most distinguished citizens.

A reporter, covering the 1937 dedication of the state historical marker in Worth's honor, wrote: "Though not a brilliant man, he was known for his sound judgment and reliability, and his opinion was sought in both legal and business affairs."

In the March 28, 1895 edition of the Asheboro *Courier*, a newspaper writer named J.R. Bulla waxed about the man in much loftier terms—and perhaps, as was typical of the day, with more than a touch of hyperbole:

When the recording angel makes up the final list of the great and good men of North Carolina—prominent and conspicuous and amongst the very first will be found the name of Jonathan Worth. He was a native of Guilford county, but moved to Randolph in early life soon after he obtained license to practice law. But Randolph claims him; he was their Jonathan Worth; they first discovered him.

Governor Worth was not only a man of grand and towering intellect, but he was a very close student—a wonderfully working man—never idle—he was not much of a believer in the triumphs of genius without industry. It is a very unusual occurrence for an astonishing head and an astonishing hand to be united in the same person, but such was true of Governor Worth.

He was conservative and far seeing in everything. A friend to education and a friend to the poor…And while he was eminently conservative he was always on the skirmish line of improvement. He was not the first to take up the new, but was not the last to throw down the old. As long as virtue, talents, learning, and kindness have an admirer the name of Jonathan Worth will be remembered. He was a great and good man.

THE STRAIGHT-SHOOTING
BEANSHOOTER MAN

Rufus Hussey was a straight shooter. He could flat-out knock a quarter out of mid air with a well-aimed rock from a slingshot.

And he could, figuratively speaking, knock a famous television talk show host down to size with a few well-placed words of country wisdom.

The low-key fellow known as the Beanshooter Man demonstrated the former hundreds, maybe thousands, of times in his life. The latter, he did but once. And once was enough for him.

Hussey was born and raised with ten brothers and sisters on a farm south of Seagrove. His father died when he was young. He learned to make and to shoot slingshots as a youngster—his oldest brother got to carry the only gun in the family—both to pass the time in the woods with his friends and to put food on the supper table.

He and his friends called the slingshots "beanshooters."

In his later years, Hussey reminisced that he first shot a beanshooter when he was six, made his first one when he was ten and even carried one while he was in the military during World War II. He returned home and settled down to raise chickens on a one-hundred-acre farm.

About 1972, Hussey got the notion to start making and selling beanshooters to the general public. Not everyone, he surmised, had been fortunate enough to learn about them while they were growing up.

Beanshooters, Hussey maintained, were history, a lost art that he planned to revive.

Making and shooting slingshots made Rufus Hussey "famous." *Rufus Hussey; Randolph County Historical Photographs; Randolph County Public Library—Randolph Room.*

And resurrect it he did, single-handedly elevating awareness about beanshooters to folks in central North Carolina and later, when reporters and television crews came calling, on the national stage.

On the first weekend of every October, the Randolph Arts Guild hosts the Fall Festival on the downtown streets of Asheboro, the Randolph County seat. The gathering was originally an arts and crafts show, tilted toward the presentation of old-fashioned activities and handicrafts.

For many years, Hussey could be found at the festival, sitting at the corner of Sunset Avenue and North Street, his vendor booth stocked with his signature beanshooters in a range of sizes. He called them "models"—the Stork model was tiny, a tribute to unborn babies, which he gave to expectant moms; the Junior, for small hands; the Derringer, sized for easy concealment in a sock; the Ladies'; the Magnum; and, the big dog of the bunch, the Hunter.

Hussey always signed (writing his initials, R.H., on the butt of the beanshooters) and numbered his work. He kept track of the serial numbers by recording numbers on the flaps of a ragged pasteboard box in his shop. The last beanshooter he made was No. 15,864.

The Beanshooter Man collected "forks" from trees, which he let air dry for months before whittling off the bark and scraping the wood clean with a glass shard. He used pure rubber gum strips from a Greensboro company and scrap leather from an Asheboro shoe manufacturer to fashion the working end of each slingshot.

He always said he used most any kind of wood, save persimmon.

"You can have one [made of persimmon] in your pocket and you can't pucker your lips enough to whistle at a rabbit to get him to stop," Hussey said, tongue-in-cheek, a twinkle in his eye. "When you get a chance at a rabbit, you want to dispatch him."

Hussey's outsized yet understated personality and fascinating craft attracted attention.

In 1986, he accepted an invitation to make an appearance on *The Tonight Show* with Johnny Carson, the king of the late-night talk show at the time. Charles Kuralt came to Hussey's Seagrove-area farm later with his *On The Road* series for CBS TV.

Getting in touch with Hussey to make such arrangements was not as easy as picking up the phone and calling. Hussey and his wife, Geneva, did not have a telephone for a long time. One reliable way to reach Rufus was to call a local pottery where his sister worked so she could relay a message. If all else failed, a person who could find Seagrove likely could find someone who could offer directions to the Hussey farm.

Hussey agreed to fly to California for the Carson show only after the TV folks told him that he could wear overalls to talk about beanshooters. Before he left for the trip, he explained to a newspaper reporter why he was going: "I want to let people see the things you can do with the things that you have—natural resources," he said. "I want to show how you can take the simple things of life and confound the mighty."

The night of the show, January 23, 1986, Hussey, wearing his usual overalls and a ball cap, sat beside Carson in his tailored suit and captivated both host and audience with his down-home conversation.

Carson said he'd heard that Hussey did not own a television set and wondered if he had ever seen the show. Hussey said that he had, one time, about a month earlier. Carson asked what he'd thought of it. When Hussey hesitated, Carson urged him to be honest.

"All I'm going to tell you—I'm going to be honest," Hussey said. Grinning, he added, "I tell you, I think there's room for improvement."

Everyone, including Carson, roared with laughter. Carson gave Hussey a point for the quip—then kept a running tally as they talked.

The Beanshooter Man told Carson that he was married to "the best woman in the world" and the oft-married TV host complimented Hussey on his belief in the institution of marriage.

"Sure I believe in marriage," Hussey said. "One time."

Carson chewed his lip.

"That's two for Rufus, none for Carson," he said.

Hussey explained that he got up every morning at five o'clock and ate breakfast at six o'clock before heading out to feed 11 cows and 12,500 chickens. Then, he said, he started his day.

When Hussey pulled a beanshooter from his sock, Carson asked if he'd like to demonstrate his talents.

"I'd rather shoot the beanshooter than shoot the bull," Hussey said.

"Three-zip," Carson deadpanned.

Hussey loaded his beanshooter with rocks that he'd brought cross-country in an old bleach container and began to shoot at targets set up on stage, zapping them with deadly accuracy. After a while, he handed Carson a stick and told him to hold it out while he took aim. Carson feigned fear, his hand shaking, and commented that the rocks Hussey was shooting were real and that they were moving really fast.

But he held out the stick. Hussey snapped it in half with a stone, and then asked Carson to hold out the half that remained. A reluctant Carson complied. Hussey hit the mark again, leaving Carson clutching a stub.

In the end, Carson took one of Hussey's huge hands in his and smiled.

"You're a remarkable man," Carson said. "Pleasure to have you."

Kuralt came calling at his home a few months later. When he shot a quarter out of the air for the camera, Hussey noted that he could do better.

"I can hit a penny," he said, "but when it gets that cheap, it's time to quit."

David Letterman, another talk show celebrity, tried to get Hussey to come to New York City for his show. He never went. The last time the Letterman people made contact, Hussey commented, in vintage form: "Doesn't he know it's deer season? I got to be out in the woods. If he wants to come down here, I'll take some time to talk to him."

Hussey was seventy-four when he died in 1994.

He died doing something he loved—felled by a heart attack while sitting at his kitchen table, listening to the radio and carving a beanshooter from a piece of oak with his pocketknife.

NO. 43, A RANDOLPH
RACING LEGEND

The King was born in, raised in and currently lives in Randolph County.

He does not wear a crown, but a cowboy hat, dark sunglasses and a trademark grin.

His domain extends to wherever stock car racing fans live.

The King, of course, is Richard Petty of Level Cross, the winningest driver in the history of NASCAR. He was a seven-time NASCAR champion, won the Daytona 500 seven times and was the first driver to pass the million-dollar mark in winnings.

He was the rookie of the year in 1959 and voted most popular Winston Cup driver nine times. By the time he retired from driving in 1992, he had taken the checkered flag 200 times—including winning 27 races in a single season, 1967. Only one other driver, Bobby Pearson, has won half that many races. Pearson won 105.

Petty edged out Cale Yarborough for his last victory, the Firecracker 400 at the Daytona International Speedway on July 4, 1984. Ronald Reagan was on hand that day, the first time a sitting U.S. president had ever attended a race.

The No. 43 Pontiac Petty was driving that day, with its distinctive red-and-Petty-blue paint scheme, is one of the objects of popular culture in the Mirror of America Collection in the Smithsonian's National Museum of American History. (Petty has said that Petty blue was "discovered" by accident when white and dark blue paint were mixed together—his crew did not have enough of either to paint an entire car.)

He received the Presidential Medal of Freedom, the nation's highest civilian award recognizing exceptional meritorious service, from President George H.W. Bush in 1992. Among the others honored the same year were David Brinkley, Johnny Carson, I.M. Pei, Ella Fitzgerald, Audrey Hepburn, Isaac Stern and Elie Wiesel.

"Welcome to the White House," Bush said in his opening remarks. "I'm going to keep this relatively short today because afterwards Richard Petty and I are going to take a few laps around the Ellipse in No. 43."

When the president knows what number car you drive, you have arrived.

But Petty did not win the medal just because he won so many races—although some race fans might make the case that his performance on the racetrack, and his personality off of it, was a primary catalyst for the meteoric rise in the popularity of the sport of stock car racing and was indeed worthy of recognition for great service to his country.

He was recognized as an American legend and an American hero who exemplified "the dreams, dedication, and drive that make this nation great."

He's a member of the North Carolina Athletic Hall of Fame and the International Motorsports Hall of Fame. In 2008, the North Carolina Motorsports Association (NCMA) honored Petty with the Achievement in Motorsports Tribute Award for his lifetime accomplishments in motorsports and contributions to the state of North Carolina.

An eight-mile stretch of U.S. 220, a four-lane highway that passes near his Level Cross home, was dedicated in his honor in 1992. The volunteer fire station near his home had taken the number "43" years earlier.

The love felt for Petty has always been returned.

"This is the center of my world," he said, speaking at the road dedication. "It's the greatest place I've ever been. There's no place I like as much as home."

Richard Petty grew up roaming the woods around Level Cross, near Randleman in northern Randolph County. His daddy, Lee, was a truck driver. He was thirty-five when he and his brother Julie decided to do some moonlighting in the fledgling world of organized racing. It was 1948 when they put a Chrysler engine in a 1937 Plymouth and Lee won his very first race.

NASCAR racing legend Richard Petty always takes time to sign autographs. *Richard Petty; Randolph County Historical Photographs; Randolph County Public Library—Randolph Room.*

Before long, Lee was taking his family—his wife, Elizabeth, and his sons, Richard and Maurice (who would later play a major role in Richard's career as an engine builder)—to races with him. Young Richard grew up yelling for Daddy on the track (and when his turn behind the wheel came years later, Richard took his family with him on the racing circuit, too).

The elder Lee passed good racing genes to his son. A three-time NASCAR Winston Cup champ, Lee won the first Daytona 500. He started 429 Winston Cup races, finishing in the top five 283 times (66 percent of his starts) and in the top ten 376 times (an astonishing 88 percent). He won 55 races, placing him number nine on the list of all-time winners.

Richard's first race was on a one-third-mile track in Toronto, Canada.

In his autobiography, Petty recalled the first race he thought he'd won.

He took the checkered flag at a track in Atlanta. Lee Petty was in the same race but did not join his son in the winner's circle. He stayed out on the track for another lap.

A puzzled Richard found out that there had been a protest: The flag had been waved early. The race official that told the younger Petty about it added that he shouldn't feel too bad about the situation.

"It's all in the family," the man said. "Your daddy's won the race."

Petty, who did not feel better, asked who filed the protest.

"Why," the official replied, "your daddy did."

Petty said he learned the meaning of "bittersweet" that day in Atlanta. The situation also served as a concrete lesson in competition.

He did not wear sunglasses as a young driver. He wore goggles. The heat combined with his perspiration caused the goggles to fog up, making it pretty hard to see. He had to change something if he planned to see where he was racing.

He tried a pair of wraparound sunglasses. They protected his eyes and did not fog up. Before he realized it, the sunglasses had become a Richard Petty trademark.

Then he started wearing a cowboy hat. When he saw pictures of himself, there was the hat.

Petty decided the hat made a pretty neat trademark, too. He still wears both.

When he was driving, Petty said, he was in another world:

> *If I went to a race and there wasn't anybody there, I wouldn't feel too racy. But after they drop the green flag, everybody could get up and go home and I wouldn't know it.*
>
> *Getting in that race car, that's the most relaxed I am. You get away from people—you're your own person. You can run fast. You can run slow. Out of the whole week, there's three or four hours I can get away from the telephone, the interviews and get on a high. It's a free spirit deal.*

It's a "deal" that runs in the family.

Richard's son, Kyle, followed in dad's footsteps and won his first race in 1979. He's still racing, but is also involved in high-profile work off the track, including the Victory Junction Gang Camp for sick children that he founded with his wife, Pattie, in honor of their son, Adam.

On April 2, 2000, at Texas Motor Speedway, Adam Petty became the first fourth-generation driver to start a Cup event. Three days later, family patriarch Lee Petty passed away. A month later, on May 13, 2000, Adam was killed in a crash during practice at New Hampshire International Speedway.

Richard Petty and his wife Lynda have served the community in a myriad of ways. They've both held elective office. She served on the Randolph County School Board for years, including time as the chair. He was a Randolph County commissioner for sixteen years. Every year, the Pettys host a fish fry fundraiser for the Republican Party at their Level Cross home.

In 1996, he made an unsuccessful run to be North Carolina's secretary of state.

"I'm not a one-dimensional person," Petty said during his campaign. "I've run seven different businesses as part of Petty Enterprises. And as a commissioner in Randolph County, I helped keep our taxes among the lowest in North Carolina. I know what it takes to run a business efficiently. That's what we need in the secretary of state's office."

An era ended in 2007 when Petty announced that after nearly sixty years, Petty Enterprises, the family racing operation in Randolph County, was moving to a shop in Mooresville. The move was necessary, Petty said, to try to keep up with the rest of the high-powered racing teams, most of which are based these days in the greater Charlotte area—and where most of the most talented crew people in the sport have settled.

"It's really, really hard to do," Petty said at the time, "plus we were so much a part of the community, it's kind of hard for us and for the people around the community to accept, 'Hey, they're not there anymore.'"

The move leaves the sixty-five-thousand-square-foot facility in Level Cross—next-door to the house where Richard Petty was born—empty. Future plans, Petty said, might include moving the Petty Museum, which is in the community center in downtown Randleman, back to the race shop where it started. Other options are to relocate the company's show car business or the Richard Petty Driving experience there.

"The big deal is," Petty said, "that no matter where we were at or whatever, when you walk through the gates at Level Cross you walked through NASCAR history. We're gonna always have this home. If we need to, we can always come back."

Just seven months later, in June 2008, Petty made another era-ending announcement—majority control of Petty Enterprises had been sold to a private equity firm called Boston Ventures. The reason? An infusion of money, big money, was needed to steer the nearly sixty-year-old family business into a more competitive position with top racing teams already fueled by corporate cash. Petty said he would play a large role in day-to-day operations.

Pick a year and Petty has probably been honored many times—2007 was no exception.

It was announced in 2007 that a new twenty-thousand-square-foot building for Autobody Repair and Automotive Systems programs at Randolph Community College in Asheboro would open in the fall of 2008. It will be named the "Richard Petty Education Center."

In 2007, Petty was one of seven men honored in Washington, D.C., as an Outstanding American by the Paralyzed Veterans of America for teaming up with driver Tony Stewart to launch a campaign for SpeedyTags. One side of each tag is imprinted with the name and likeness of a major name in racing, like Petty or Stewart, and the reverse shows support for paralyzed veterans. The purchase of a tag supports the organization that is dedicated to fighting the nation's paralyzed veterans and all people with disabilities.

"I feel very strongly that we must support our brave men and women returning from Iraq and Afghanistan injured," Petty said, "and I don't think there is a person in America who doesn't stand behind our troops and thank them for their service. This is one small way fans can join me in supporting our paralyzed veterans."

Petty accepted the G. Lynn Nisbet Award from the North Carolina Travel Industry Association in 2007 on behalf of Petty Enterprises "in recognition of outstanding contributions that have developed the travel industry in North Carolina by raising the national profile of the state as a destination."

Tammy O'Kelley, director of the Randolph County Tourism Development Authority, nominated Petty Enterprises for the honor. "For as long as there has been NASCAR, there has been Petty, the only family that has had four generations to race in the sport's highest level," O'Kelley said when introducing Petty during the award ceremony. "Today, the Pettys' influence, both on and off the track, has endured."

And likely will as long as there is racing.

Or a worthy cause.

THE "MOTHER" OF THE SOUTH'S BAPTIST CHURCHES

The penetrating gaze of Elder Shubal Stearns, a Yankee missionary, is represented in a round memorial stained-glass window—"the eye of Shubal"—in the present-day sanctuary of Sandy Creek Baptist Church.

The church is on Sandy Creek Church Road, off of NC 49 a couple of miles south of the town of Liberty in northeastern Randolph County.

According to the writings of church historian Morgan Edwards, who was at Sandy Creek in 1772, Stearns also possessed a "musical and strong" voice that he employed "to make soft impressions on the heart, and fetch tears from the eyes."

Edwards recorded the following memory, from a man named Tidance Lane:

> When the fame of Mr. Stearns had reached the Yadkin, where I lived, I felt a curiosity to go and hear him. Upon my arrival I saw a venerable old man sitting under a peach tree, with a book in his hand, and the people gathering about him.
>
> He fixed his eyes upon me immediately, which made me feel in such a manner as I had never felt before. I turned to quit the place, but could not proceed far; I walked about, sometimes catching his eyes as I walked. My uneasiness increased and became intolerable.
>
> I went up to him, thinking that a salutation and shaking hands would relieve me, but it happened otherwise. I began to think he had an evil eye and ought to be shunned, but shunning him I could no more effect than a bird can shun a rattlesnake when it fixes his eyes upon it. When

he began to preach, my perturbations increased, so that nature could no longer support them, and I sunk to the ground.

Stearns's manner in the pulpit was a revelation. "The message of the preacher, in a word, was a simple gospel, easily understood even by rude frontiersmen," wrote Dr. William L. Lumpkin in his book, *Baptist Foundations in the South.* He continued:

Pungent words and homely illustrations made vividly clear some of the profoundest religious ideas. The enthusiastic manner of the preaching, too, was unprecedented. Stearn's delivery was warm and appealing, full of persuasive zeal, not at all the commonplace, lecture-type discourses which the people had formerly heard. Strong gestures and a fervent plea told the people that the preacher was intensely involved in his message. It was obvious he wanted a verdict.

This two-century-old church building has shed its siding and been restored.
Sandy Creek Baptist Church; Randolph County Historical Photographs; Randolph County Public Library—Randolph Room.

Elders Walter C. McMillan, L.D. Cashion and Gurney Nance, November 15, 1953. Sermons were delivered from this pulpit. *Sandy Creek Baptist Church; Randolph County Historical Photographs; Randolph County Public Library—Randolph Room.*

The music in the little pastor's voice soon penetrated every heart, and his piercing, discursive eye seemed to peer into every soul. The tears, tremblings and shouts of the members quickly affected the visitors, and from the little meetinghouse a tumult of grief at sin and joy at salvation ascended to heaven.

Stearns's preaching and presence produced profound results that reverberate throughout the twenty-first century.

Born in Boston in 1706 and raised as a Presbyterian, Stearns was converted in a great revival led by George Whitefield about 1740 and became a member of the New Lights or Separates. He was baptized in 1751 and headed south to spread the gospel, stopping first in Virginia before moving on to settle at Sandy Creek.

The Massachusetts native and fifteen followers organized Sandy Creek Baptist Church in the autumn of 1755, meeting in a brush arbor while building a log meetinghouse near the creek at the conjunction of two roads, one leading northwestward to Salem and southeasterly to Fayetteville, the other heading south to Cheraw, South Carolina, and north to western Virginia.

Within three years of its founding, Sandy Creek's congregation had swelled to 606, and two more churches, Abbot's Creek and Deep River, had been established.

In 1758, Stearns led in the establishment of the Sandy Creek Association, the oldest Baptist association in North Carolina and the third-oldest association in the United States. For the next twelve years, all Separate Baptist churches in the Carolinas and Virginia were affiliated with this association.

By 1772, when Morgan Edwards set down his account, 42 churches and 125 ministers "had sprung from the parent church." A plaque on a twelve-foot-tall obelisk dedicated at the church's bicentennial in 1955 tells the story this way:

> *On this site, in November–December 1755, Rev. Shubal Stearns, his wife, and those who came with him, seven other families, 16 souls in all, built their first meeting house, where they administered the Lord's Supper.*
>
> *It is a mother church, nay a grandmother and a great grandmother. All the Separate Baptists sprang hence, not only eastward towards the sea, but westward towards the great river Mississippi, but northward to Virginia, and southward to South Carolina and Georgia. The word went forth from this Sion, and great was the company of them who published it in so much that her converts were as drops of morning dew.*

For years, a state historical marker erected near the church in 1938 recognized Sandy Creek with this inscription: "Mother of Southern Baptist churches. Founded 1755, by Rev. Shubael Stearns, whose grave is 2 mi. S." The marker was changed in 2001 to read: "Mother of Separate Baptist churches across the South. Founded by Shubal Stearns, 1755. His grave is two miles south."

To some, the differences have little meaning. But to others, those distinctions are important.

To understand, one must know that the oldest Sandy Creek church building still standing, a log structure built around 1802, is situated between two churches—the Sandy Creek Church and the Sandy Creek Primitive Baptist Church.

Both active church families are descendants of the mother church.

According to a history of Sandy Creek, published on its 250th anniversary, church records record how members of the church Stearns founded parted ways:

> *In 1830, a protest arose by some of the members of Sandy Creek congregation concerning the support of missions and the new institutions being formed by the newly organized Baptist State Convention, causing a split in the church. The members who were opposed to the missionary movement of the Convention continued to hold services at the original site, and adopted the name of Sandy Creek Primitive Church…*
>
> *The members who desired to support the missions program and the Sunday School ministry of the Baptist State Convention sought out a new location. They settled near a school known as Shady Grove and continued to be known as Sandy Creek Baptist Church. Then in 1905, some of the descendants of those who had left, under the leadership of W.H. Eller, returned to the original location, and once again established worship services.*

The congregants who returned to the original church site kept the name Sandy Creek Church. The church established in 1830 then became known as Shady Grove Baptist Church.

In 2005, Hal Younts, church clerk of Sandy Creek Primitive Baptist Church, noted that the highway marker had been wrong for decades on two accounts. The first, Younts said, is that his church is directly descended from the church Stearns founded, and it is not a Southern Baptist church. The second mistake, he added, was that Separate Baptists did not call their leaders "Reverends," referring to them as "Elders."

Younts spent years painstakingly restoring the old log church, replacing rotted logs and reinstalling a balcony that was torn out in the 1920s. Some of the logs he replaced had to be hewn by hand because they were too long—about thirty feet—to be done at a sawmill.

Stearns is buried beside his wife Sarah in the cemetery owned by members of the Sandy Creek Primitive Baptist Church.

In his book, Dr. Lumpkin assigns Stearns and his followers a prominent position in Baptist history: "The accomplishments of the Separate Baptist movement are extremely remarkable since Baptists prior to 1755 were an insignificant and generally despised sect in America."

On Shubal Stearns Day in 1955, Dr. Henry S. Stroupe, a history professor at Wake Forest University, paid tribute, too: "We honor him today," Stroupe said, "for his work in making religion vital and real in a frontier region whose religious influence had been little felt prior to his time."

And that religious influence reverberates today. "All the Baptist churches throughout the South," Younts said, "regardless of what faction they are, are sprung off from Sandy Creek."

A DARING DEED
OF FAITH

In 1928, the Daughters of the American Revolution gathered at a bridge over the Deep River in the town of Franklinville to dedicate a marker.

The plaque honored Revolutionary Patriots of the area in general and a Patriot named Andrew Hunter in particular.

According to the bronze marker, in the year 1781, Hunter rode a horse down a steep rock about two hundred yards downriver (and in sight of the bridge) to escape from the close pursuit of a Tory named Colonel David Fanning and his men.

The daring escape (whether or not it ever took place) led to a name for the place: Faith Rock.

In the Franklinville area of Randolph County, the tale of Hunter's feat is legendary; at least twice, residents celebrated "Andrew Hunter Day" with a horse and pony show, and a nearby road is named after him.

It was long said by some local tellers of the tale that a visitor who examined the rock with great enough care would find hoofprints, indentations etched in stone by Hunter's horse as the fleeing man and his surely frightened steed plunged pell-mell toward the water, and potential freedom, some sixty feet below.

The version of the story commemorated by the DAR seems to meld two tales told by Dr. E.W. Caruthers in a book published in 1854. The Franklinville legend goes something like this.

Fanning was a Tory, one of the colonists who sided with Great Britain during the Revolutionary War. He was a man with a reputation as a

This landmark earned its name Faith Rock thanks to a story of a daring escape. *Faith Rock; Randolph County Historical Photographs; Randolph County Public Library—Randolph Room.*

ruthless marauder who, with a band of followers, carried out campaigns of burning and killing in Randolph and Chatham Counties.

He discovered Hunter, a man he had sworn to kill if he ever captured him, hiding in a wagon. Instead of dispatching the Patriot immediately, the Tories took time to eat some food that was also hidden in the wagon. While they were distracted, Hunter leaped onto Fanning's horse, an exceptional mare named Bay Doe, and fled.

When Hunter reached the rock, flight seemed futile. Yet his options were to be captured and die or direct the horse down the sheer rock face and grasp a chance, however small, to live. Hunter gave spurs to the mare.

Some said the Tories who witnessed the daring ride were so amazed that they did not fire a single shot; others said shots were fired, but that the Patriot escaped unscathed.

In his book, Caruthers tells of two actions involving Hunter and Fanning that took place in the Little River-Deep River section of Moore, Randolph and Montgomery Counties in North Carolina.

The North Carolina preacher's florid prose paints Fanning as a fearful villain possessed of qualities quite larger than life: "With the astuteness of the Indians and the fleetness of the Arab, with a constitution capable of bearing any amount of toil and with patience, hunger and fatigue worthy of any cause, he might be said to be always on horseback and always in motion, often appearing upon his enemies when they least expected it and accomplished his purpose of death and destruction."

The minister wrote that Hunter escaped from Fanning on Fanning's favorite horse, Bay Doe. Caruthers wrote that Fanning gave orders to his men to "kill the rascal but save the mare" and that Hunter was shot in the shoulder as he fled. Hunter saw blood on the mare and thought it was she that was wounded. He realized that he was hurt but kept riding until he reached the home of a friend many miles away. His friend sent for a physician and Hunter recovered.

On another occasion, according to Caruthers, Bay Doe saved Hunter's life as he was being pursued by some of Fanning's men "on the high ground south of Deep River." With no options, Caruthers wrote, Hunter rode the horse down a precipice some fifty feet into the river.

A telling of the story by Fanning himself does not mention a rock. After the British defeat, the Tory leader fled, and, in 1790, when he was living in Canada, wrote about his "adventures" in North Carolina from 1775–83. Hunter was shot two times as he galloped away on Bay Doe, Fanning wrote, "with my saddle, holsters, pistols and all my papers of any consequence to me." He recorded nothing about the Patriot escaping by riding down a rock.

Instead, he wrote, he went to Hunter's plantation: "I took his wife, three Negro boys, and eight head of horses. I kept his wife for three days in the woods; and I sent the man to see if he would deliver up my mare, and property, containing my papers." Hunter sent a letter, according to Fanning, saying that he was sick and begging for the return of his wife.

The missive directed Fanning to keep the Negroes and horses until his horse could be returned to him.

Still other versions of the story say encounters between Hunter and Fanning took place far from Randolph County.

One of those accounts, which is included an 1867 book entitled *History of the Old Cheraws* by Bishop Alexander Gregg, says that Hunter escaped from Fanning in the Drowning Creek (Lumber River) region of southeastern North Carolina. Gregg wrote that the horse Hunter was riding when he was captured was named Red Doe. He escaped on Fanning's mount, which he rechristened Red Buck. Gregg did not write about a rock.

Another says that Hunter's escape occurred in the Mars Hill section of Florence County in South Carolina. That version, an addendum by a man named R.J. Blackwell, appears in the republished edition of Gregg's history, issued in 1925. Blackwell wrote that his version corrected Gregg's "erroneous" story.

According to Blackwell, Hunter was captured close to his home near Mars Bluff and then leapt onto Fanning's prized mare, Red Doe, while the party of Tories was eating breakfast. Hunter jumped Red Doe from a high bluff near Mars Bluff into the Pee Dee River and escaped to safety on the river's eastern bank.

In no account does Fanning recapture the mare. For many years, some horse owners in the Randolph County area proudly (whether truthfully or not) traced the ancestry of this or that animal in their possession to the heroic mare, Bay Doe.

What version of the story is true?

No one knows.

In 1975, James A. Rogers, the editor of the *Florence Morning News*, wrote a series of columns exploring the differing accounts. In the final installment, Rogers wondered whether Hunter had escaped on Fanning's mare in the Mars Bluff section of South Carolina as local legend had long claimed.

"The answer," Rogers wrote, "is possibly 'yes' but probably 'no.'"

In the end, he concluded, there was really little point in trying to uncover the true story of Hunter and Fanning:

If true believers consider it intellectual mischief to tamper with a cherished legend, they have a point. Unless it does history an injustice, why not indulge belief and enjoy the romance of it? It is a valid question for which we really have no answer.

The truth is we'll continue to be thrilled by Red Doe streaking away from David Fanning with Andrew Hunter leaning forward on his withers and leaping headlong from a high bluff into the Pee Dee River near Mars Bluff.

And Randolph County residents will continue to be thrilled by the image of Hunter—and a horse named Bay Doe—plunging to freedom down a rocky precipice into the Deep River near Franklinville.

They will keep faith in Faith Rock.

TRINITY—THE ROOTS OF A GREAT INSTITUTION

Duke University's roots reach all the way to nineteenth-century Randolph County and reveal a succession of predecessors: Union Institute; Normal College; and Trinity College.

Dr. Brantley York and the Reverend Braxton Craven, a pair of Randolph's native sons, steered the institution for its first forty-four years. Each stands as a pioneer of education in the Old North State.

The people of northwestern Randolph County invited York, a teacher and preacher, to move to their community to oversee Brown's schoolhouse, a one-room log cabin with a wood chimney and a dirt fireplace. They offered him $200 a year, a house to live in and wood to burn.

York accepted the offer, arriving in the spring of 1838 with a reputation for being able to solve problems using plus and minus signs and for being able to read Latin and Greek. Within a year, he had sixty-nine students; within two years, the school was upgraded twice, first to a better log building, then to a two-room frame structure.

He persuaded the local folks to organize an educational society with dues and a governing board. He named the school Union Institute, a tribute to the collaborative efforts of Methodists and Quakers to form a successful school.

In 1842, York moved on, launching more academies, publishing textbooks and preaching. He established subscription schools, named York Institutes in his honor, all over North Carolina, teaching grammar, a smattering of math and the New Testament. He was later the president of Rutherford College, where revival services complemented the schoolwork in preparing young men for the ministry.

York wrote in his autobiography that the driving force in his life had been battling ignorance and wickedness. Dr. E.C. Brooks of Duke University credited him with success on at least one front: "No one man has lived in our state," Brooks wrote, "who did more to arouse interest in improving the mind."

When he was thirty-seven, York lost his vision in one eye. Thirteen years later, he became blind in the other. But he kept working. In his lifetime, he taught more than fifteen thousand students and presented more than eight thousand lectures and sermons.

A young man named Braxton Craven from the Buffalo Ford section of southeastern Randolph arrived as a pupil at Union Institute when he was about twenty. Soon, York employed Craven as an assistant teacher. He took over upon York's departure and marshaled the school for forty years, until his death in 1882.

Craven, an orphan who rose to acclaim as one of the most respected men in the state, never forgot his painful past. In one of his addresses to the students at Trinity, Craven gave this counsel:

> *In all your ways, let me entreat you, remember the orphan by day and by night; his is a hard, oh, it is a bitter lot! There is much more poetry than truth in the world's pretended kindness to the poor, sorrow-faced little boy that has no mother to love him and no father to protect him.*
>
> *He is sorely oppressed in his boyhood; he may dig himself a home in the mountain granite, but orphan haunts him like a midnight ghost. In his manhood, the lingering curse of his sad condition rests upon him. The world has no cavern to shield him from the opposition.*
>
> *I have seen the tears flow as if the fountains of his soul were broken up, and have seen him bow before God and ask for love to bind up his broken heart, and I have seen the cold combinations of this world grind him to powder. Always, my young friends, have a kind word for him and treat him as a brother.*

In about 1848, Craven initiated a program of teacher training; convinced of the importance of such training, he lobbied for the support of state government. He had facts to bolster his request.

A report to the General Assembly of North Carolina in the early 1850s contained some distressing statistics: of 3,000 teachers in the state, the report said, "2,000 cannot teach English grammar, 1,800 are deficient in geography, 1,200 cannot teach the whole of ordinary arithmetic, 1,000 can scarcely make up a readable return." State lawmakers passed a bill rechartering Union Institute to create Normal College, the first college in the South chartered with the authority to issue licenses to schoolteachers. Within a year, the roll numbered 152 students.

A few years later, Craven sought the support of the North Carolina Conference of the Methodist Church. In 1856, the conference adopted the school and took ownership of the property. In 1859, the church assumed complete control of the college and the name was changed to Trinity, after the famous college in Cambridge, England.

In 1890, historian J.A. Blair wrote that Trinity "is a neat little village in the northwestern corner of the county, is well and tastefully arranged, and takes its name from the College."

For a brief time during the Civil War, Craven organized students into a company called the "Trinity Guards," who guarded prisoners of war

Duke University had its beginnings near this spot in northwestern Randolph County. *Trinity College; Randolph County Historical Photographs; Randolph County Public Library—Randolph Room.*

while they were in school. Enrollment fell as students went off to war. The college closed its doors for nearly a year in 1865 and 1866. Confederate troops pitched their tents on the school grounds. An ordained minister, Craven left the school to serve as pastor of a Raleigh church.

Difficult days lay ahead when the school reopened in 1866, but by the school year of 1869–70, enrollment climbed to two hundred. Another gloomy period followed several years of prosperity. When Craven died, some feared that Trinity would not survive.

The Methodists, the community and others who believed in the school stepped up to keep the institution afloat. Another Randolph County native, Marquis L. Wood, served as interim president; he was a graduate of Normal College, an ordained minister and a former missionary to China. Five years later, in 1887, Wood returned to the pastorate and a Yale graduate named John Franklin Crowell arrived as president. The same year, Trinity received its first donation from a Durham tobacco manufacturer named Washington Duke, who gave $100,000.

In 1888, the college president coached the school's new football team to victory in its first game, beating the University of North Carolina in a contest played in Raleigh.

Once again, school enrollment rose.

The new president and others soon came to the conclusion that the college could not serve its greatest usefulness or reach its great potential in the little village of Trinity. Local protests met a proposal to move the college to an industrial center, but bids were solicited from various cities in the state. An offer from Raleigh—twelve acres, $20,500 in pledges and the promise to raise more money—was accepted.

Then Durham made a better offer: $85,000 from Washington Duke and a sixty-acre park on the western edge of town from Julian S. Carr, a longtime Trinity College trustee.

The cornerstone of the main building was laid in Durham's Blackwell Park in 1890. After the tower of the college's one new building came crashing down in 1891, operations came back to Trinity for one more year. School opened in Durham in September 1892.

The final name change was reported in the December 14, 1924 issue of the Raleigh *News and Observer*:

The eyes of the nation were turned toward Trinity college last week when James Buchanan Duke with one single stroke of a pen proposed to give that institution six million dollars outright for new buildings and to give it forever one-third of the income from a forty million dollars trust fund.

Already the most richly endowed educational institution south of the Potomac river, this new equipment and additional endowment will make it one of the most richly endowed educational institutions in America.

There is to be a school of liberal arts or whatever the academic department of a modern university is called that will continue to be known as Trinity College, which is to be an integral part of what will be known as Duke University. Fond recollections linger about the name of Trinity, and the sons and daughters of the old college will not willingly see it die.

In 1977, the old Trinity High School building, erected in 1925 on the site of the original Trinity College building (which was condemned and razed in 1924), was slated for demolition. The building contained materials from the old college's main building.

John Lawrence, who was superintendent of Randolph County schools at the time, wrote Duke President Terry Sanford and suggested that it might be a good time to erect a marker commemorating the origins of the university.

In October of 1984, the Trinity College Memorial Gazebo was dedicated on the grounds of Braxton Craven Elementary School in Trinity. (A state roadside historical marker at Braxton Craven School also commemorates the school history.) The columns supporting the roof once supported balconies in old Trinity High School, and before that they served a similar function in the main building of the old Trinity College. Iron urns once marked the entrance to the Trinity campus. The centerpiece is the old Trinity College bell, which was removed from the Duke Chapel tower. Two of the original ten columns were exchanged with Duke for the bell, to be used in a historical shrine on the Duke campus.

Brantley York is buried in the cemetery at Rocky Springs Methodist Church in Alexander County.

Braxton Craven is buried in Trinity Cemetery, established in 1859 to bury a student who died of typhoid fever.

ST. PAUL—A HISTORIC CHURCH, A HISTORY MUSEUM

S t. Paul Museum would be a Randolph County treasure even if it did not already contain treasures.

Located at the intersection of Stout and High Point Streets in Randleman, the building that houses the museum was the first brick church built in the county.

An interior designer named Jule Körner painted the interior of the sanctuary at St. Paul Methodist Episcopal Church. Körner, working under the trade name Reuben Rink, was a nineteenth-century character, as revealed in his home in Kernersville, North Carolina, in Forsyth County. The house, called Körner's Folly, has twenty-two rooms on seven levels, with ceilings ranging from six feet to twenty-five feet tall. (It is open to visitors for walk-in tours; there is an admission.)

The talented fellow made Bull Durham Tobacco Company famous by traveling around the South painting advertisements featuring a bull. During the weeks that he and some coworkers stayed in Randleman, they were not painting bulls, but decorating the interiors of private residences as well as the stately church.

Unfortunately, Körner's artwork has faded, leaving whispers of images on white plaster walls. There are no known pictures of what the walls once looked like. In his 1985 book, *The Architectural History of Randolph County, North Carolina*, author and architectural historian L. McKay Whatley paints a picture with words:

"At the church," Whatley wrote, "Körner expanded on the theme of the single pointed arch stained glass window behind the pulpit to create a triumph of trompe-l'oeil interior design: a marble Gothic cathedral in paint and plaster."

Restoration, or even recreation, of Körner's work would be expensive, but it's still a dream, according to Louise Hudson of the North Randolph Historical Society, which was organized in 1966 with two purposes: to restore the church and to establish a historical museum in it.

"One of these days we may run across some kind of technology that will let us clean the walls and restore the artwork," Hudson said.

Painted on opposite sides of the arched recess behind the pulpit are the Ten Commandments and the Lord's Prayer. Historical society members say they do not know if the fancy lettering is the handiwork of Körner's crew or someone else.

A stained-glass window in the recess was dedicated to John H. Ferree, one of the brick church's benefactors, after his death in 1889. The window depicts two angels whose wings seem to be ablaze when the sun is at a certain angle in the afternoon; one angel holds a staff decorated with faceted glass "jewels."

The house of worship was distinguished by a couple of other features: a balcony that wrapped around three sides of the sanctuary, planned, it is recorded, to seat the servants of church members, and a ceiling painted robin's egg blue. Tradition says that the building's red bricks were fired in a nearby kiln using hand-pressed clay dug from the property.

Ferree and John Banner Randleman financed construction of the church, which was built on the site of the first church, a wood structure. The brick church cost about $4,000. The men owned a mill on the nearby Deep River. Both are buried in the cemetery that wraps around three sides of the church.

The town, formerly Union Factory, took the name Randleman when it was incorporated in 1880. Randleman's elaborate monument stands some fifteen feet tall.

"To his genius and energy the Deep River Manufactories are indebted for their magnitude and importance," read the words etched into his marker. "The piles of stone and brick, the turning wheels, the hum of spindles, the clash of looms, the towns that dot the River banks, are his monuments."

Randleman may not have lived to see the church completed. He died at age fifty-one on July 12, 1879, the same year the new church's

The oldest brick church in the county now houses a museum. *St. Paul Museum; Randolph County Historical Photographs; Randolph County Public Library— Randolph Room.*

doors opened. St. Paul Church was used as a place of worship until 1947, when the congregation merged with the members of Naomi Falls Methodist and built a new church (the present-day First United Methodist Church) downtown.

After that, the church was used for a few funerals and a few weddings, but the historical society—with its mission to save it—bought the old building for a dollar from the West North Carolina Conference of the United Methodist Church in the 1960s.

The museum owns a lectern, an altar chair and a table that were in the church when it took possession, but area residents donated most of the collection—an eclectic mix of memorabilia, some of it from

Randleman and some from the surrounding area. Most of the items are from Randolph County.

Support for the preservation effort has waxed and waned over four decades, but society members have been careful to protect the building with a new tin roof, new windows and a new steeple. The steeple was funded via print sales of a picture of the church painted by Randolph County artist Carol Robbins.

The balcony rail has been restored. A reproduction of an altar rail visible in an old photograph of the church interior was crafted and installed in the early 2000s.

One of the more interesting historical treasures in the church is a two-horse hearse. Originally owned by Jesse Pugh, the hearse is more than a century old. The conveyance was stored for years in a southern Randolph County barn, until Jesse's son, Jack, loaned it to the museum. It is still equipped with some of its original fixtures—black shades and timeworn velvet curtains that were once drawn over the windows during funeral processions.

When the hearse arrived, it would not fit through the front door. A crew of men took the wheels off and handed the hearse in through an open window.

The museum has many photographs, newspapers and letters of historic significance. Other notable items in the collection include an old loom; a 1940s-era Boy Scout uniform; a doctor's medical bag, also from the 1940s; an assortment of old-time hand tools (including a maul, a fro and an auger); farm equipment and machinery (such as a scythe and a mechanical winnower); a piece of molding from an old stagecoach inn that stood in the early 1800s on what is now U.S. 311, in proximity to the community of Sophia; and a lock from a courthouse at Johnstonville (a crossroads community created by the state legislature in 1788).

"We have," Hudson said, "a fairly good cross-section of life."

The museum is typically open to visitors on the third Sunday of every month, except in January, February and March, when it is open by appointment only. Admission is free. Contact: North Randolph Historical Society, P.O. Box 1341, Randleman, North Carolina, 27317; nrhs@stpaulmuseum.org; or 336.495.1128.

EVERGREEN ACADEMY, A SCHOOL BUILT BY QUAKERS

A simple, single-story building at the intersection of Peace Haven and Hinshaw Town Roads in eastern Randolph County offers no indication that it is historic.

But it is.

The wood-frame structure, in what is known as the Holly Spring community, housed the first school that opened in that part of the county after the Civil War ended. It was called Evergreen Academy.

Its days of operation were brief—from 1867 until the early 1880s, when the county's public school system had been reestablished—but the school filled a need during a critical time. The academy served students who had missed several years of schooling while the conflict raged.

Area schoolchildren sometimes make field trips to the old academy, but most passing motorists probably pay little attention to the nondescript building.

The rectangular structure has no underpinning, but stands on large stones. Inside, partitions, both permanent and movable, divide the school into two large rooms. Recitation platforms, about eight inches high, flank each end of the academy, and the interior walls on each end are painted black, making "blackboards." A visitor can still see the "ghost" of decades-old chalk markings on those walls.

A Quaker group called the Baltimore Association to Advise and Assist Friends in the Southern States provided most of the funding for the school, with help from Friends in England, Scotland and elsewhere. Local Quakers, with few resources after the war, donated what they could to the

When the Civil War ended, children needed a school to attend, so the Quakers built this one. *Evergreen Academy; Randolph County Historical Photographs; Randolph County Public Library—Randolph Room.*

project—mostly trees for lumber and labor to see the school rise from the ground. Holly Spring resident Thomas Hinshaw deeded a tract of land on which to build the school.

Seth Hinshaw, a grandson of Thomas Hinshaw, published a booklet about the school in 1994. He wrote it, he said, to preserve the story of the importance of the school and the work of the Friends who established it.

Hinshaw quotes from a book entitled *Quaker Contributions to Education in North Carolina* by Zora Klain: "The contribution that North Carolina Quakers made to education does not lie so much in the number of schools that they established…but in their attitude toward education, and in their active stimulation of the community interest in schools."

Frances King, a wealthy Baltimore businessman who helped lead the formation of the Baltimore Association in 1865, made forty trips to North Carolina to supervise the group's work there. Hinshaw wrote:

"He was in the Holly Spring community many times, conferring with Thomas Hinshaw and others about the urgent need for a school in the community."

Minutes of the Holly Spring Monthly Meeting, dated 1866, state that "the Meeting authorizes the Committee appointed in 11th month to build a school house if the necessary subscriptions can be raised and report to this Meeting when complied with."

Teacher pay came from the subscriptions and from tuition paid by students who lived outside the community, according to Hinshaw. Friends in Philadelphia and London supplied some books; other books were left over from a school operated by the Holly Spring meeting before the war.

The schoolhouse also served as a community center, hosting events from spelling bees to evangelistic meetings. In an autobiography, Anna Winslow, a traveling California evangelist, wrote that she had meetings at Evergreen schoolhouse in 1885 and again in 1887.

In another booklet he wrote, a 1989 publication featuring facts and folklore about Hinshawtown, Seth Hinshaw speculates on why an evangelist would set up shop in a school instead of a meetinghouse.

"Most likely," he wrote, "Holly Spring Quakers at the time did not want a revival in the meetinghouse, and a schoolhouse seemed more appropriate. It is a little surprising that Thomas Hinshaw even allowed this."

When the academy ceased to operate, the building was used for six-week "subscription summer schools" to supplement the county school term, which was just three to five months long. Those sessions lasted until about 1910.

Thomas Hinshaw bought the school and the acre of land it stood on from the meeting in 1915. For about fifty years, it was used for grain storage. These days, it stands empty.

Seth Hinshaw wrote that he considered the Evergreen Academy to be a landmark:

> *Insofar as I know, it is the only building of its kind still standing intact in the South...In retrospect, it is obvious that Evergreen Academy had a comparatively brief period of service, from 1867 until the early 1880s, except for the many subscription summer schools following. The*

important fact is that it filled a vacuum for a generation of children who would have been without the opportunity of going to school.

The brevity of its period of service may have caused it to be too often overlooked in the annals of Southern Quakerism.

"LITTLE CHILDREN...
CORRECTLY TAUGHT"

The Asheboro Female Academy, one of Asheboro's most historic buildings, gains little everyday notice.

It stands within spitting distance, some might say, to one of the busiest intersections in town—the corner of Park Street and Walker Avenue, a corner which sees quite a bit of traffic daily during the school year. Asheboro High School stands on one side of Park and South Asheboro Middle School on the other (with the middle school fronting Walker Avenue).

The old academy, a single-story frame structure, stands alongside Walker Avenue, across from the middle school, hidden in plain view behind the city schools' offices. Those who know the place exists probably pay the small, tidy building little notice as they drive past.

But the school attracted quite a bit of attention in its day.

Back in the nineteenth century, when the school opened, there were so many students after a year that an assistant was hired and the "infant class" was moved to the nearby Methodist Church.

An article in the August 1960 edition of *Southern Architect* magazine, in a section on North Carolina's historic buildings, spotlighted the Asheboro academy:

> *The city's first piano was bought for the Female Academy and music was an important part of the genteel pursuits in which the students were instructed. Tuition charges were made separately for spelling and reading, arithmetic and history, music and instruction in the making of wax flowers and fruit.*

Girls finally had a place to go to school when the Asheboro Female Academy opened in 1839. *Asheboro Female Academy; Randolph County Historical Photographs; Randolph County Public Library—Randolph Room.*

The formation of a Female Academy in Asheboro—a complement to the Male Academy that stood at the corner of Fayetteville and Academy Streets—was formally announced in the February 8, 1839 edition of an Asheboro newspaper called the *Southern Citizen*:

> *The friends of female education (and we hope there are many) in this section will be gratified to learn that the citizens have agreed and pledged and obligated themselves to erect a Female Academy. A suitable building to be commenced forthwith.*
>
> *As the benefits to be derived will extend through a section heretofore destitute, and considering that we are mostly mechanics and merchants of moderate capital and limited income—consequently not well prepared to raise funds for public enterprise, it is confidently hoped and believed that our fellow citizens in this and neighboring counties will be pleased to extend to us such aid as may be within their power.*

A local merchant named Colonel Benjamin Elliott donated $400 and an acre of land on which to build the school. The site, known as Elliott's

Green, is the present-day location of Randolph Bank at the intersection of Fayetteville and Salisbury Streets. Five years earlier, Elliott had given two acres of land across the street to the Methodist Episcopal Church for construction of a church and public cemetery (the city cemetery that stands there today).

The school opened about four months later. One room in the academy, an 18½-foot-by-36-foot structure, was reportedly large enough to accommodate sixty students; the piano stood in a second room, which also served for depositing hats, bonnets, cloaks and a small collection of books.

Old records show that tuition for spelling and reading for a five-month term was six dollars, for arithmetic and history, seven dollars. Music tuition was twenty dollars. Some city residents boarded students for six dollars a month.

An unnamed visitor to the school in November 1839 penned a glowing review, which reads, in part:

> *The Trustees have been as careful and as liberal in procuring a Teacher as they have been in building and providing the house. They have employed a Lady from Boston of first rate qualifications. I had the pleasure of hearing her exercise some of her classes—and was delighted to perceive that she is fully competent.*
>
> *The first class she examined consisted of some small ones who had commenced 4 months ago in the Alphabet. They could read, and read correctly. They spoke loud, pronounced each word with distinctness, and after they had concluded the reading of their lesson, the tutoress gave out to them some of the most difficult words in the lesson, and they spelled them correctly—giving a distinct articulation to each letter and syllable. I never saw little children so correctly taught.*

Both the male and female academies were closed to students during the Civil War. They housed soldiers instead.

Public education gradually improved after the war and private schools were absorbed into the state's education system. So, both Asheboro academies closed. The sale of the Female Academy helped pay for an Asheboro graded school at the intersection of Fayetteville and Academy Streets.

The school building was moved to the west end of the same lot to make way for a home built by banker W.J. Armfield Jr. It was converted into living quarters for servants, and then later used for storage.

In 1969, Armfield's descendants offered to give his old two-story home and the old academy to the Randolph County Historical Society for use as a headquarters and museum. That deal fell through three years later when a suitable agreement could not be reached on what would happen to the property if the historical society could not maintain it—historical society members wanted the deed to contain a clause that would convey the property to the City of Asheboro in such an event; the descendants required reversion to the family.

The old house was demolished in 1973. The Armfield family gave the Female Academy to the historical society, along with $17,500 and a five-acre tract of land on Uwharrie Street. (The land was subsequently sold to Union Carbide.)

The academy was moved to its Walker Avenue location after school officials agreed to lease the property for ten dollars a year. A dedication of the building, which had been refurbished inside and out, was held in November 1976.

Historical society members have been working for several years to pave the way to move the Female Academy once more, to a vacant lot at the southeast corner of Salisbury and Main Streets. Besides offering a more central location in the city, the intersection is historic. It served as the city's courthouse square in the nineteenth century. Another historic structure, the Marmaduke Robins law office, already stands alongside Main Street. That small frame building, which even hosted some town commissioners' meetings in the early twentieth century, dates to circa 1860.

CENTRAL SCHOOL—PRIDE, LOVE AND LEARNING

The winds were right for change in 1926 when students moved from the ramshackle Asheboro Colored Graded School at the intersection of Burns and Greensboro Streets to a spanking new structure called Randolph County Training School on Watkins Street.

In fact, about three months after the transition, wind blew to the ground the rickety, three-room wooden structure where black children had studied since 1911.

The new brick school was built with Rosenwald Funds, moneys from a foundation established by Julius Rosenwald, a part owner of Sears, Roebuck and Company, to assist public education, Jewish charities and African American institutions.

From its inception, the school was the focal point for activities in the black community.

It served students in Asheboro and far beyond, since the only other school in Randolph County open to black children at the time was in Liberty, a town in the northeastern corner of the county.

Several former teachers and a former principal shared memories of the school during interviews in 1986.

J.N. Gill served as principal of the school in its golden years. He took the job in 1946. Two weeks before school began, he walked up and down the corridor of the white high school on Fayetteville Street in Asheboro, surveying stacks of classroom materials for the upcoming year.

He saw new supplies for every school in town except for his—and he asked why.

When he was told there were none, he again asked why.

No one had ever requested any, he was told.

Over the next fourteen years, Gill filled out a truckload of requisition forms to get books and other supplies to educate his students.

When he took the job, the school had no cafeteria and no gymnasium. When it was time to play or practice basketball, students had to move chairs out of the auditorium. Eight grade levels of younger students were crammed into four rooms and a wooden building known as "the Chicken Coop."

In the late 1940s, four classrooms, a home economics department and a lunchroom were added to the original building. Later, an eight-room elementary building was constructed, and finally, in the 1950s, a gym.

Gill recalled being instrumental in the construction of the first lighted football field for blacks in the state of North Carolina. He explained that he was persistent in asking permission for his players to use Lindley Park, the field for white students, scheduling practices and games when the white team did not need it.

"I pestered 'em so much about using Lindley Park," he said, laughing, "they bought land and put lights to it."

Central School had a ball field but no bleachers. Before every game, Gill said, he sent his coach over to Lindley Park to dismantle stands, bring them to Central and reassemble them. Then the bleachers had to be back in place at Lindley Park before they were needed again.

"They got tired of that, too, and bought us some bleachers," he said.

James D. Morgan Jr., the school's first band director, remembered taking his young charges from Randolph County Training School to a band festival in Greensboro. Though the students had only been practicing for seven months, they earned a rating of excellence.

They were also labeled as "bad boys and girls."

The school name led the other participants to assume that Morgan's students hailed from a reformatory in Asheboro. The children were crushed.

"We've got to change the name of this school," Morgan told McGill as soon as the band returned home.

With his principal's blessing, Morgan visited the office of Guy B. Teachey, the superintendent of the city schools, and told him the same thing.

When the school's name was Randolph County Training School, some people thought that its band members were talented juvenile delinquents. *Central School; Randolph County Historical Photographs; Randolph County Public Library—Randolph Room.*

"Well, what do you want to change it to?" Teachey asked.

Central School, Morgan replied. And, simple as that, the name was changed.

Morgan and his students had picked the name because the city of Asheboro sat smack in the center of the state.

In addition to band, Morgan taught math, physics, chemistry and biology. And, since there was no period devoted to band, he had to steal time for music instruction wherever he could find it—during recess, at lunch, after school—one on one, one on two, one on four or one on eight. Sometimes the entire group assembled in the auditorium.

They had no uniforms at first, but wore white shirts with black trousers, ties and shoes, topped off with jazzy, white "be-bop" caps Morgan bought at a department store. Much later, the band got smart black-and-white uniforms.

Morgan was a stern taskmaster, demanding diligence and devotion to practice from his players. But he tempered his demeanor with a dose of paternal love. He instilled a sense of self-worth in his pupils by addressing them as "Mr." and "Miss."

"It made 'em have a little pride," he said, "and you just don't know what that meant to them to have a little pride."

Some told Morgan he was wasting his time trying to teach "slow learners" how to play an instrument. Morgan would smile at doubting Thomases.

"Would you mind if I try?" he would say.

Then he would set to work.

> *I admit some of 'em couldn't learn at the same speed. But, I'd ask them to come after school, on Saturday mornings. When they finally caught on, when they learned to read those lines and spaces of music, they caught on and went like fire.*
>
> *There is no such thing as can't be done. If you have the time and the patience and the love, it can be done.*

Ruth McRae was in the eighth grade when classes moved to the new school. Years later, she came back to teach third and fourth graders. Her ties to the school go back even further: Her grandfather, Zachary Franks, was a minister and brick mason. He was selected by members of the Odd Fellows Lodge to lay the cornerstone for the new building.

She recalled teaching during a time when the supplies were hand-me-downs from the all-white schools.

"We had very few advantages," McRae said, "nothing much in our school but books, but we very seldom had children who couldn't read and write and do a little bit of math when they finished."

Mabel Patterson also attended the school, graduating two years after the move to the new building, and returned to teach there for twenty-five years. She remembered students carrying chairs down the dirt street from the old school to the new school and noted that something to sit on was practically all the facility had in the way of amenities.

She shared space with a fifth-grade teacher in a cramped, two-room building and was teased, good-naturedly of course, by other teachers for giving up a job in a perfectly good school in another town to return home to teach in "a chicken coop." Teachers who needed to use a dictionary, she said, had to bring one from home.

The school's first library was housed in the elementary school addition.

"In that library we had old books that had been transferred" from the white schools, Patterson said. "Some of them would be out-of-date. It really wasn't much of a library, we just fixed it up."

Since there was no school lunchroom, Patterson said, teachers often sent students to pick up lunches from a "cafeteria" operated by a woman who lived a few houses down the street. Sometimes, she said, students would come running back with the food, wide-eyed.

"Oooooh, Mrs. Patterson, I saw that lady fanning flies in her kitchen— there were so many flies," a child might say.

Patterson cringed at the memory.

"It hasn't been easy," she said.

Revitalizing the property in east Asheboro following a period of disuse and abuse was not easy either. Integration of public schools led to the closing of Central High School in 1965; the elementary school was closed three years later.

The buildings stood unused for years, except for a period when the Randolph County Sheltered Workshop and the Randolph County Department of Social Services occupied the elementary facility. They eventually moved to new quarters.

By the late 1970s, the property was in shambles, its buildings empty, padlocked and posted with "No Trespassing" signs; windows were boarded up or broken out. In 1981, a nonprofit group called the East Side Improvement Association achieved a longtime dream by purchasing the Central property for $32,000. Their dreams called for renovating the old school buildings and gym to create a recreational and cultural center, once again making the site a hub for members of the community. Initial plans called for the creation of a nursery/child care center, an adult day care and a place for youth activities.

More than a quarter of a century (and more than $2.5 million in renovation expenditures) later, the old high school now houses East Side Homes, an apartment building for low-income, elderly residents; the former elementary school houses Asheboro Day Care Center, a nonprofit, neighborhood-based day care center; and the gymnasium is home to the Central Boys & Girls Club, featuring a gym, a learning center, a technology center, an arts and hobbies area, a kitchen and outdoor recreation areas.

And, a testament to its rebirth, the property is listed on the National Register of Historic Places.

THE REBIRTH OF A "KISSING BRIDGE"

A historic bridge stands in southern Randolph County. Sort of. Only part of it is the original bridge, but its story of survival is certainly historic.

The Pisgah Covered Bridge in the Pisgah community ten miles southwest of Asheboro is a reconstruction of a forty-foot wooden bridge that was originally built by J.J. Welch about 1910.

Legend has it that Welch was paid forty dollars to build the bridge over a branch of the Little River. Travelers used the covered bridge until a new road and a modern bridge were constructed in the 1950s.

The new road bypassed the covered bridge, but many people did not.

For decades, the landmark was a destination for history buffs, bridge lovers and lovers in general, as well as people who enjoyed the little getaway just off the beaten track.

The bridge may be one of the most oft-painted scenes in Randolph County.

More than one couple exchanged wedding vows at the scenic spot.

Covered bridges were called "kissing bridges" because young fellows could steal kisses—away from prying eyes—as they passed through the dark passages in buggies with their sweethearts. But covered bridges were not built with romance in mind. Roofs kept timbers from rotting and provided shelter for travelers.

Randolph County once had more covered bridges than any of the state's other ninety-nine counties; as late as the 1930s, the county still boasted fifty-one covered bridges in use.

The original Pisgah Covered Bridge washed away, but this replica should be able to survive a one-hundred-year flood. *Pisgah Covered Bridge; Randolph County Historical Photographs; Randolph County Public Library—Randolph Room.*

In fact, the county was once home to a great number of bridges, covered and otherwise. A 1972 article by Henry King in the Asheboro *Courier-Tribune* credited an Asheboro man, Dr. J.S. Pritchard, with holding precise views as to why so many man-made spans crossed Randolph's rivers, creeks and streams. According to the good doctor, there were two reasons.

One was that Randolph was such a progressive county and its leaders wanted to improve communications. The second reason was less lofty: "This county has always been close politically, so candidates running for office competed with each other in pledging to build bridges."

By the 1970s, only three covered bridges remained in the Tar Heel State. Two were in Randolph County: the Pisgah Bridge and the Skeen's Mill Bridge, which was west of Asheboro.

In 1970, North Carolina Governor Bob Scott announced the allocation of $35,000 to preserve the Skeen's Mill Bridge, a one-hundred-foot-long span over the Little Uwharrie River. At the time, there was speculation that the bridge might be moved to a state park, possibly to William B. Umstead Park near Raleigh. That move, however, never came to pass and the Skeen's Mill span was washed away in a heavy rain in the mid-1980s.

That left two—the Pisgah Bridge, which has always been easily accessible to the public, and the privately owned Bunker Hill Covered Bridge, which stands two miles east of Claremont in Catawba County. This ninety-one-foot-long bridge over Lyle's Creek was built in 1894 as an open span; it was covered in 1900 and restored in 1994. In 2001, the Bunker Hill Bridge was designated as a National Civil Engineering Landmark.

Then came a violent storm on the night of August 10, 2003. Winds blew and waters beneath the bridge swelled higher and higher, fourteen feet above normal, it was reported later; finally, a piece of Randolph County history which had survived Hurricane Hazel in 1954 was washed and blown away.

The next day, all that remained of the Pisgah Covered Bridge were its stone foundation pillars. Pieces of the bridge were scattered downstream and throughout the woods; some even came to rest in the tops of trees.

Before the sun went down that day, plans had been announced to refurbish a hiking trail and footbridges that had been built four years earlier when the bridge was restored through a collaboration of the North Carolina Zoo, the North Carolina Zoo Society, the North Carolina Department of Transportation, the Piedmont Land Conservancy and the LandTrust for Central North Carolina.

By week's end, the scope of the project had expanded.

Zoo director David Jones announced that an outpouring of public support gave proof that the bridge itself, which he called "a Randolph County icon and a significant state landmark," in addition to the trails and footbridges, could be restored.

"Using the salvaged pieces," Jones told a reporter for the Asheboro *Courier-Tribune*, "we must be certain that it is rebuilt to resemble the original bridge as closely as possible. But we must also build a structure that will not be washed away again."

Some pieces of the bridge were never recovered. As news about the bridge spread the morning after the storm, many people headed to the site to reminisce. Unfortunately, some of them were souvenir hunters and took pieces of the bridge home.

Others were less selfish: Jones reported during the rebuilding effort that enough lumber dating from the early 1900s had been offered to restore every covered bridge that once stood in Randolph County.

Cash and in-kind donations of nearly $80,000 covered the restoration of the bridge, nature trail, picnic tables and walkways and established a trust fund for future maintenance.

The new bridge—built to withstand a one-hundred-year flood, which authorities say is what felled the original span—was dedicated in April 2004, nine months after the storm.

It is an amalgamation of wood salvaged from the original structure (more than 90 percent of the pieces salvaged were utilized), aged wood from tobacco barns donated by area farmers, concrete and steel.

But visitors do not see concrete and steel. Reinforced concrete piers are faced in traditional stone; the sixty-foot-long steel beams that support the bridge are encased in wood.

Longtime visitors to the Pisgah Covered Bridge were accustomed to a tin roof. The roof of the rebuilt bridge is hand-split wooden shingles of Northern red cedar. Researchers say the original bridge had a wooden roof, which was replaced during the Great Depression. William Moffitt, the local contractor who supervised the rebuilding project, also noted that as the shakes age, they will turn gray and match the original wood.

The Pisgah Covered Bridge is open to visitors every day. It costs nothing to stop and take a picture, have a picnic or enjoy a leisurely stroll along the quarter-mile hiking trail.

COURTING HISTORY IN THE COUNTY SEAT

T is a tale of two courthouses—and two monuments—in downtown Asheboro, the county seat of Randolph County.

The majestic old Randolph County Courthouse, which opened in 1909, faces Worth Street.

Out front of it is a tall monument, topped by a bronze-cast Civil War soldier.

Just a short way to the east stands the Randolph County Veterans Memorial, which was dedicated in 1995.

Not far from the Veterans Memorial is the new Randolph County Courthouse, a four-story structure of beige brick and green-tinted windows. It opened in 2002.

THE OLD COURTHOUSE

When county officials decided in 1908 that it was time for a new courthouse—one with a fireproof vault for record storage—they dispatched the chairman of the board to Iredell County to see *its* new courthouse. He was allotted eighteen dollars for expenses.

City life had pulsated around the courthouse at the intersection of Salisbury and Main Streets until a train depot was built on Depot Street (now Sunset Avenue) in 1889. Businesses sprang up around the station.

Many wanted a new courthouse to be built near the depot.

Others wanted it to remain where it was.

The old Randolph County Courthouse opened in 1909; the monument in front was dedicated in 1911. *Randolph County Courthouse; Randolph County Historical Photographs; Randolph County Public Library—Randolph Room.*

Commissioners compromised. They picked a site in between—Dr. John Milton Worth's old cornfield and barnyard on Worth Street. A group secured an option to buy the property for $3,400, but A.C. McAlister and his wife later donated the land.

A group of lawyers bought a strip of land 40 feet wide and 150 feet long next to the new courthouse site for new offices. They paid $1,300 for the plot and built what became known as Lawyers' Row.

County officials instructed the architects, hired at a cost of $300, to model the Randolph edifice after the one in Iredell.

The new three-story courthouse featured 700,000 yellow bricks and granite trim. It cost $34,000. Construction started in 1908; the first court session was held in July 1909.

An annex was added in 1950 at a cost of about $100,000; a second annex, with two courtrooms, was built in 1981.

The old courthouse stands empty in 2008 while county officials decide how to best put the historic structure to use.

AN OLD MONUMENT

The statue was dedicated on September 2, 1911, by Randolph County Daughters of the Confederacy at a cost of $1,700. The monument honors nine groups of Randolph County soldiers who fought in the Civil War.

Zell Brown, a twenty-four-year-old horse trader, transported the monument the three blocks from the depot to the courthouse using his wagon pulled by a four-horse team. He was the only man in town with a wagon long enough for the job. In later years, Brown ran a gas station not far away, at the intersection of Worth and Fayetteville Streets.

Workers built scaffolding and used ropes to attach the statue atop the twenty-foot-tall granite base. When they had finished, the monument stood twenty-eight feet and ten inches tall.

The unveiling was an all-day affair, with most festivities held on the grounds of the Presbyterian church across the street. Walter Clark, the chief justice of the state supreme court, was the featured speaker. Bands played. Children decorated the monument with laurel wreaths.

For nearly eighty years, the soldier stood sentinel, facing south, though most Rebel statues dotting the South defiantly face north, according to *The Architectural History of Randolph County, North Carolina* by Randolph County attorney, historian and writer L. McKay Whatley.

Then the Confederate soldier lost a skirmish with Hurricane Hugo when it swept through Randolph County in September 1989. The hurricane had been downgraded to a tropical storm by the time it blew into Randolph, but with wind gusts of up to forty miles per hour it still felled some trees and power lines.

When workers arrived at the courthouse the next morning, they found the soldier hanging by one foot from atop the granite base. And so, the statue got an unofficial name:

"We've decided we're going to name this Confederate soldier Hugo," said Alice Dawson, clerk to the county commissioners, on that day.

A Seagrove-area man named Ad Vanderstaak repaired and restored the statue. The fall damaged its rifle and broke one foot. Vanderstaak also cleaned it, returning it to a beautiful bronze color instead of the green and black that it had turned over time.

Vanderstaak explained that the wind knocked the statue over because an armature inside had corroded—so the hollow soldier, which weighs just eighty pounds, was no match for the storm that gave it a name.

A New Memorial

The Randolph County Veterans Memorial was dedicated on Veterans Day, November 11, 1995, to recognize Randolph veterans who served in the military from World War I through Persian Gulf action.

About 1,500 people gathered in heavy rain and blustery wind for the occasion.

Frank Rose, head of the Randolph County Veterans Council, spearheaded the effort to establish the memorial, which featured the names of more than 3,300 who had served in the twentieth century in World War I, World War II, Korea, Vietnam, Grenada, Lebanon and the Persian Gulf; and the names of 90 killed in action. More names were added a year later.

Two new granite panels—and more names—were added to the Veterans Memorial in 2005.

The new panels featured the names of 544 military personnel (with space for 1,300 more names), bringing the total number honored on the memorial to 3,899.

A New Courthouse

After two years of construction, the new four-story, 89,969-square-foot Randolph County Courthouse opened on July 1, 2002. The total cost of the courthouse project, which included design and engineering fees and restoration of a 1981 addition, was approximately $16 million.

Banks of green-tinted windows (eleven feet wide and twenty-four feet tall) ring the beige-colored brick structure. Some of the windows provide panoramic vistas of downtown Asheboro for those in offices or lobbies. Some of the windows simply mask blank walls.

The new building boasts seven courtrooms and offices for the county clerk of court, the district attorney and district and superior court judges.

Security was foremost in courthouse design.

All visitors enter through the front door and pass through metal detectors. Fifteen cameras around the courthouse, both inside and out, monitoring activity. With the touch of a button, a deputy can zoom in on a vehicle in the parking lot close enough to read the license plate number. A computer system monitors more than thirty secured doors in the building. An unauthorized entry appears on a monitor screen in red letters.

The initial plan was to design a building that would serve the needs of a growing population for a quarter of a century. Due to fiscal concerns, that vision was scaled back to accommodate needs for fifteen years.

The design anticipates expansion.

The entrance is off-center, but with a forty-eight-foot addition to the west side of the courthouse, the doors would be smack in the middle of the building.

One artifact links the old courthouse with the new one. It's a bell, encased in the second-floor lobby.

In 1838, the bell was brand new; it hung in the belfry of the courthouse at the intersection of Salisbury and Main. It was cast in a foundry in Medway, Massachusetts, established in 1816 by a man named Major George Holbrook, who, as a youth, apprenticed under Paul Revere in the machinist and clock-making trades.

When the courthouse was moved in 1909, the bell was moved, too—hoisted into housing in the attic. A rope attached to the bell dangled through a hole in the pressed-tin ceiling over the balcony in the third-floor courtroom. One of the duties of the janitor was to climb into the gallery and pull the chord to open and close court.

The 200-pound, 24½-inch-diameter bell was removed by a crane from the 1909 courthouse and restored at a cost of $7,500 by Morton Dark Jr. of Siler City. Dark used a brush and then dental picks to remove sap that had dripped and solidified onto the surface of the bell before applying three coats of automotive-grade, clear-coat lacquer.

AN ENDURING PRESIDENTIAL "ENDORSEMENT"

A presidential boost for an Asheboro company half a century ago still has the place rocking.

P&P Chair Company makes the famous Kennedy Rocker, though that is not what the company called it back in 1961, before news broke that President John F. Kennedy kept one of the rockers in the Oval Office as an antidote for an aching back.

Before the nationwide exposure, the chair bore a simple designation in the P&P catalogue: the No. 1000 Jumbo Rocker, and accounted for about a quarter of the company's sales.

It was March of 1961 when Kennedy's White House physician, Dr. Janet Travell, told reporters how much he liked the high-backed wooden rocker in his office. Dr. Travell declined to name the North Carolina company that manufactured the chair, but said she would be glad to tell anyone who wrote and inquired.

She was deluged with requests.

The first day after the story was published about the rocking chair, she received fifty letters. The next day, she got five hundred.

After Kennedy was elected to lead the nation in 1960, men across the country trimmed the lapels of their coats because the charismatic young president wore his lapels narrow.

Folks clamored for a rocking chair like the president's, too. Sales more than tripled.

"We hardly know where we stand," company cofounder W.C. Page Sr. told a Raleigh newspaperman one day in late March 1961. "I've been

Nearly half a century after the public found out that the president had one, people still want a Kennedy Rocker. *P&P Chair Company; Randolph County Historical Photographs; Randolph County Public Library—Randolph Room.*

up day and night for two days, handling telegrams, calls and letters from Maine to Florida and Manteo to Milwaukee. We could hardly get into the plant this morning for the cars and trucks waiting there."

Today, model No. 1000 is the only chair the company makes. It is available with a woven cane seat and back, like Kennedy used, or with a seat and back of slats, in a variety of finishes.

The chairs are produced in the same unassuming metal building, using the same techniques and even some of the same equipment utilized to make the first rockers in 1926, when W.C. Page and Arthur E. Presnell started the company. The two buddies, who had worked together in an Asheboro furniture factory before joining the service, first discussed their business in the trenches of France during World War I.

"That's when I and a friend began thinking and dreaming about going into the chair business on our own," Page told a newspaper reporter from Greensboro in 1961.

Company owners have never marketed the woven-back chair as the Kennedy Rocker, although that is what it's still called by many people. They call it the Carolina Rocker, a trademark name that can be found stamped under the arm of each genuine P&P chair, because that's what Kennedy's physician called it.

In a 1961 newspaper interview, W.C. Page said Dr. Travell first ordered rockers from his company in 1953.

"In her letters requesting more chairs for her patients," Page recalled, "Dr. Travell always called the rocker the Carolina rocker, and that's what we are calling them today, the Carolina rocker."

Kennedy, who had suffered a back injury during World War II, really liked the chair in Travell's New York office so he asked her to get him one.

An eight-page spread in the April 1961 issue of *Life* magazine explored the fine pleasures and healthful benefits of rocking. In the article, Travell praised the P&P product as "a really good rocker, one that fully supports the back. Such a chair provides gentle, constant exercise and helps prevent muscular fatigue."

Page passed on what the good doctor had told him.

"Dr. Travell told us that she liked our chairs because of the bent back posts which make the cane back fit the contour of a person's back. She also likes the Carolina rocker because the armrests are not too high and the detachable seat gives more support."

After Kennedy was elected as president, his personal secretary called Asheboro and ordered several of the rockers to be shipped across the country to various places frequented by the president, so that his Oval Office chair would not have to be moved every time he left town. First Lady Jacqueline Kennedy had the Oval Office chair refinished with a dark stain and ordered cushions for the arms, the seat and the back.

"Up until a few weeks ago," Page told a reporter in 1961, "all the rockers were finished in natural light oak, but when the president painted his we began putting a dark antique finish on the chairs so they can be used indoors."

The company started selling an upholstered version of the rocker, too.

Articles about the Kennedy Rocker appeared in other national publications, such as *Time*, *Newsweek* and even *Popular Science*. The company was featured on the *CBS Evening News* with Douglas Edwards. W.C. Page's brother, W.S. Page, was a mystery guest on the popular television program called *What's My Line?*

Just a few days before the firestorm of publicity thrust the firm into the national consciousness and one of its offerings to the top of many shopping lists, P&P Chair Company had curtailed operations, laying off about half of its fifty workers because business was slow.

"We don't know what the future holds right now," Page told an Asheboro reporter, "but we certainly hope that we can do something about the unemployment picture in this town and county."

As orders poured in, company officials faced a different problem— finding enough cane weavers to meet production demands. In October of 1961, Page noted that many older residents who were skilled in the art of weaving had come to the company's aid, and that the company had also enlisted the services of handicapped workers through Goodwill Industries in Winston-Salem, who were doing much of the weaving.

Later U.S. presidents wanted chairs, too, including Lyndon B. Johnson and Jimmy Carter.

When Terry Sanford was North Carolina's governor, he sent a rocker with a brass nameplate to each of the other forty-nine U.S governors.

Tom Brokaw ordered a rocker. So did Oprah Winfrey.

In a 1988 interview, W.C. Page Jr. said business was still good.

"We manufacture and sell more than we ever have," he said. "We ship to every state except Hawaii. It's a good old comfortable chair. But it's just a plain old-fashioned Southern porch rocker. We've never pretended it to be anything else."

The Carolina Rocker Kennedy used in the Oval Office is displayed at the John F. Kennedy Presidential Library and Museum in Boston, along with other items from his office, including a plaque, given to Kennedy by

Admiral Hyman Rickover, bearing an old Breton prayer, and a sterling silver goblet made in Dublin in 1805. The people of New Ross, Ireland, gave Kennedy the goblet and a White House gardener put a fresh flower in it every day. New Ross was the port from which Kennedy's great-grandfather, Patrick Kennedy, set sail for America.

P&P Chair Company is still a family business, under the management of Bill Page, the grandson of the company's cofounder.

"I guess we could have changed the way we did things, bought new high-tech computerized equipment or built a new building," Page told Tammy O'Kelley of the Randolph County Tourism Development Authority for an article posted in the "Newsroom" on the organization's website (www.heartofnorthcarolina.com).

"But it just wouldn't be the same. We're making a chair that will basically last forever. Why would we want to change the way we build it? That's what's made it special and I think that's a big part of why our rocker has remained so popular and stayed in such demand over the years. It's about authenticity. You can't get another one made like this anywhere else but here."

The famed rocker has commanded some eye-popping prices.

During an auction of property from Jackie Kennedy's estate in 1996, two of the rockers brought almost a half-million dollars. Each.

Not bad for a chair that carried a retail price of twenty-five dollars (thirty-five dollars for the dark-stained edition) at the time of the initial Kennedy publicity. Today, the retail price may range from two hundred to three hundred dollars.

People even make special trips to Asheboro to purchase a rocker. The company does not offer retail sales, but an outlet business operates out of the P&P office that sells "seconds," when available, at reduced prices.

"The average person probably wouldn't think of this company as a tourism asset in the traditional sense of the word," said tourism director O'Kelley, "but people visit Randolph County for the sole purpose of purchasing an authentic Kennedy Rocker."

A BATTLE FLAG
FINALLY COMES HOME

The Randolph Hornets—soldiers of Company M of the Twenty-second Regiment of the North Carolina Militia—marched off to war in 1861 carrying a red-white-and-blue regimental flag.

For more than one hundred years after the final shots of the Civil War, the silk banner was missing in action. The flag returned home in 1968 and has been displayed ever since at the Asheboro Public Library on Worth Street.

It is stored between pieces of glass in an anodized aluminum frame, so both sides can be viewed. The frame is set on a base made of fruitwood.

Like Old Glory, the 150-year-old flag has bars and a field of stars. There are three stripes—two red and one white—and eleven stars on what was once a blue background. It measures fifty-five inches by thirty-five inches. On one side, in two-inch-tall letters, are the words "RANDOLPH HORNETS." On the other side are three-inch-tall letters that read "ONWARD TO VICTORY." The letters were written by hand in ink or paint. A fringe rings the flag's perimeter.

In 2002, experts who examined the stained and faded flag said it needed extensive restoration work, after which it should be maintained in a temperature- and humidity-controlled environment. A piece of fabric draped over the case these days keeps sunlight from doing more damage.

The flag's homecoming began when a letter, dated August 30, 1965, arrived at the local chamber of commerce office. The post from Dr. Marian B. Roberts of Hillsborough, inquired whether Asheboro or Randolph County had a historical society.

A benevolent doctor made sure a Randolph County artifact was returned home. *Hornets Flag; Randolph County Historical Photographs; Randolph County Public Library—Randolph Room.*

"In a few days," Roberts wrote, "I hope to have an article that should be bery [*sic*] interesting to the people of your county: i.e. over one hundred years old."

"At this point, I should like you to know that I am not in the selling business; I have nothing to sell therefore this should remove any money motive if it now exists," Roberts continued.

The letter stated that Roberts had been a resident of nearby Montgomery County for a time in the 1930s and that he had made friends with several Randolph County physicians.

In September, the county librarian, Charlesanna Fox, replied that there was a historical society with headquarters in the new Asheboro Public Library, and that a section of the library dedicated to local history was called the Randolph Room.

Roberts responded immediately, first explaining that he was a longtime Civil War buff whose father had served in the Confederate army. Then he delivered the news about his article of interest:

After some four years of dickering back and forth (as Andy Brown and King Fish would say) I have finally been able to secure and have at this time in my office a flag—same flag I am sure really belongs to Randolph County. I worked through a friend of mine in Nashville, Tennessee and he through someone in Pennsylvania; from there on to New Jersey and from there I finally was able to get this flag from a person in Conn.

I must admit that I have debated with myself for some time trying to convince same that I should keep this flag but have decided that it is now time for the flag to go home to good old Randolph to be preserved from now on.

It was evidently made by the ladies of your county over a hundred years ago and went off to the war with "The Randolph Hornets."

He described the flag as "a very beautiful thing and quite delicate" and offered to personally bring the flag to Asheboro and give it to the historical society—if that group would promise to have it treated and framed professionally.

"No wonder you are excited about the flag!" Fox wrote back. "Its history is most interesting, not only the history of the flag but of your efforts in securing it."

She promised to get back in touch as soon as she was able to find out how much it would cost to do the work the doctor wanted and then find a way to pay for it. It would be nearly three years before a representative of the Randolph County Historical Society picked up the flag from Dr. Roberts in Hillsborough for transport to a Statesville furniture company that built the frame that houses it.

The framed flag was on view during a historical society meeting in September 1968 and placed on display in the Randolph Room the following month. So, the flag was home, but there was still the mystery of where it had been for one hundred years, and how it wound up so far north.

At the request of those who wanted to preserve the story of the flag, Dr. Roberts wrote about his quest and sent it to Asheboro. He again detailed the chain of people involved in the transaction, most of whom he did not know.

"I still do not know who had the flag or how it got to Connecticut," he wrote. "I have an idea it was captured."

Dr. Joseph Suggs of Asheboro wrote an article for the May 1969 issue of *Our State* magazine:

> *The company fought in every battle except First Bull Run and sustained its greatest losses at Chancellorsville, Va. After Jackson's death at this battle, Lee reorganized his army into three corps. At Gettysburg, the Randolph Hornets were a part of Iverson's Brigade, Rhodes Division, Ewell's Corps. These men were ordered to make a large sweep and assault of the Union line behind a stone wall. Heavy losses were again suffered.*
>
> *A few Hornets were present at the final surrender at Appomattox, Va., but no one knows at what time in the company's eventful career the flag passed from its possession. When next we hear of it, nearly a century later, it was located in Connecticut.*

And there the story might have ended, save for the chance discovery by Barbara Newsome Grigg, who worked at the Asheboro library, of an article in the *Weekly Times* of Philadelphia, Pennsylvania. Dated December 20, 1879, the article contains the recollections of Oliver C. Cooper, a Union soldier stationed on the northern bank of the Potomac River, the focus of an attempted blockade by Southern forces in March 1862. Confederate troops had established "formidable batteries" along the river, aiming to cut off water communication by federal soldiers with Washington.

> *On Tuesday, March 9, the unusual movements about the rebel batteries attracted the attention of our people. During the forenoon one of the gunboats—the "Anacosta," I think—cautiously approached the upper battery, dropping shells into the works as she moved down. Getting within close range and finding no signs of occupation, a detachment of men landed from the gunboats, who scrambled up the steep embankment, and soon the multitudes of our soldiers who, from the opposite river banks had been anxiously watching these proceedings, saw the Stars and Stripes wave out to the breeze above the hostile guns, and then such a roar went up as had never before rolled over the waters of the Potomac.*

Later, Union soldiers scoured encampments from which Confederate soldiers had hastily departed, Cooper wrote. They found many "relics" and almost every man went away "loaded." Among the pickings were regimental papers, reports, private letters, cooking utensils and a litter of bloodhound pups.

Cooper added this: "Two handsome banners were obtained in one of the camps—one, of silk, having belonged to an Arkansas company and the other, of satin, bearing on one side the inscription, 'The Randolph Hornets,' and on the other, 'Onward to Victory.' A building was found containing fifteen or twenty ready-made coffins, and the numerous graveyards, filled with fresh graves, which were met with, showed that sickness and death had been busy in the Confederate Camps during the winter."

THE SMALLEST "CHURCH" IN NORTH CAROLINA

There's no officially sanctioned designation certifying that the little building next to Kelly Lee's home south of Asheboro is the state's smallest sanctuary.

Nor does there need to be.

A tape measure (or the naked eye if there's no measuring tape handy) and acknowledgment by passersby that they've never seen anything quite like it are enough to tell the story.

The wood-frame structure is just eight feet by twelve feet. It looks like a playhouse that someone decided to adorn with a miniature steeple. Four pint-sized pews nearly fill the place, even though each pew is barely big enough to seat an adult or maybe two small children.

The little building bears a big name, Memorial Cathedral, a grand moniker that is faintly visible in faded letters on a sign out front. Kelly Lee said that he's been told that his Memorial Cathedral is the smallest sanctuary in North Carolina that was ever used for an official ceremony.

In fact, the tiny church has seen several. Three or four couples have chosen the child-sized chapel alongside the two-lane blacktop as the setting to exchange wedding vows.

At one time, it was commonplace for visitors to stop by the little church and disappear inside for a few moments. Some may simply have been curious about the tiny structure with a copper cross on top; others, undoubtedly, sought solitude, a place to pray, to meditate or to think. Visitors from as far away as Germany signed a guest register Lee used to keep in the chapel.

Kelly Lee built a child-sized "church" beside his home to honor his former father-in-law. Many stop here to meditate while some have wed at the church. *Courtesy of Paul Church.*

The steeple-topped structure features four miniature pews, a lectern and a handmade wooden cross. Windows are imitation stained glass. *Courtesy of Paul Church.*

But few people, it seems, know about or remember the little out-of-the-way Randolph County church anymore.

Lee built the church in tribute to his former father-in-law, the Reverend Wilburn Williamson, a fellow who had not only served as an inspiration to Lee, but had also been something of a father figure to him.

By Lee's account, the Reverend Williamson, who died in April of 1979, spoke in a slow-as-molasses drawl that left a listener wondering whether the man would ever finish a sentence. But Williamson employed the deliberate speaking pace only in casual conversation. Put the good Baptist preacher in a pulpit and he was a changed man.

"He'd start preaching and it was just like running a rabbit," Lee said in a 2002 newspaper interview. "I associated him with his religion—and he had it—and I thought, 'What can I do?—I can build a little church.'"

Lee keeps a journal, one for each year dating to the 1950s, in which he records the daily happenings in his life and in the world around him—when his three children started school, the number of the school buses they rode, when it snowed, when the Veterans Memorial was dedicated in downtown Asheboro and more.

One entry, for a Tuesday in early August 1979, reads simply: "9:20 a.m. I started building my little church today." He had finished it by August 14.

A rustic wooden cross hangs on the back wall of the chapel, behind a lectern on which there is a King James Bible. Lee crafted the cross from pieces of a walnut tree his father planted when he was a boy at the family homeplace in Chesterfield, South Carolina. The Holy Book belonged to Lee's son, Timmy, when he was a boy. The floor is carpeted and the ceiling vaulted, with exposed wooden beams. Imitation stained glass, now cracked with age, covers the four tiny windows.

The Reverend Williamson lived just a short piece down the winding road from where the little church stands. Perhaps the reverend would have liked the notion that Lee built a "cathedral" in his memory, and perhaps not, but surely he would be pleased to know that the door to the chapel still stands unbarred, as it always has, offering brief respite to all who pass.

To get to Memorial Cathedral from Asheboro, turn off Dixie Drive (U.S. 64) onto Brower's Chapel Road, and then turn right onto Pine Hill Road. The chapel will be on the right.

IT'S SHOWTIME FOR A
SHOWPLACE ONCE AGAIN

When Asheboro Mayor David Jarrell said he wanted to see the Sunset Theatre serve as the crown jewel of the city's downtown revitalization, he was recalling his boyhood days.

Back then, he could spend a mesmerizing Saturday at the theatre for just a quarter—the cost of a show and a box of popcorn.

"In those days," Jarrell said, "you could sit through a movie again when it finished. They didn't make you leave. So that's what most of us did. We'd see it twice."

City officials bought the old five-thousand-square-foot movie house for $250,000 in 2005. They made the purchase from the George Washington Carver Community Enrichment Center—the modern-day descendant of Asheboro's George Washington Carver College that operated during the 1940s for the area's black residents.

Members of the nonprofit group had bought the landmark five years earlier with plans to develop it into a performing arts center for the community. The project proved to be too costly.

They asked the city for money and received an allocation of $10,000 for programming.

In the end, city officials decided that the best way to save the historic structure was to buy it. The theatre building includes a small storefront on either side of the theatre proper. The one to the east was last occupied by the Little Castle restaurant, another longtime landmark downtown; the building to the west last housed a beauty salon. There was once a barbershop in that building, with showers in the basement. Many customers once stopped by the barbershop for a haircut, shave and shower.

The city subsequently bought two buildings beside the theatre, too, so there would be plenty of space to develop it properly—room for a larger lobby, handicap-accessible bathrooms and perhaps dressing rooms and storage space and such.

The Sunset Theatre was the first building in the city that was built solely as a motion picture theatre.

Built in the Spanish Colonial Revival style popular in southern California at the time, the Sunset was a showplace when it opened on March 6, 1930.

W.P. (Dick) Stone managed the theatre during its glory days.

Announcement of his promotion appeared in the November 14, 1941, issue of the Asheboro *Courier-Tribune*: "Mr. Stone's promotion is well deserved," stated the front-page item. "He started out with Mr. [J.F.] White when the Capitol theatre opened on December 19, 1922, as sound technician and projection man, and has been with Mr. White ever since. When the Sunset theater was opened on March 6, 1930, Mr. Stone moved over to that place, but still kept a technical eye on the Capitol."

When Stone trained that "technical eye" onto the Sunset on a full-time basis, he orchestrated the goings-on more like a Broadway show producer than a movie theatre manager, wrote Bob Williams in a 1985 story in the *Courier-Tribune*.

He dressed in a dark suit, dark necktie and a dark wide-brimmed hat and usually carried a big cigar.

"He would open the theater about 1 p.m., clean things up, then walk back to our home on Cranford Street where he would shower, put on his Sunday best, then walk back to the theater," Stone's daughter, Emily Redding, told Williams in 1985.

"He would stand out front of the theater, dressed like an undertaker, and shake hands with everybody who bought a ticket. He saw his role as host and official greeter."

He sometimes assumed the role of censor, too.

When movies began to get more explicit in the 1960s, Redding said, her father would simply retrieve a pair of scissors and go to work on segments he deemed inappropriate:

The Sunset Theatre was the first building in Asheboro that was constructed solely as a movie house. *Sunset Theatre; Randolph County Historical Photographs; Randolph County Public Library—Randolph Room.*

He would go up into the projection booth and cut the dirty parts out of the films. It made for some hilarious scenes on the screen. You would see the couple headed for the bedroom door and the next thing you knew they were standing out in a pasture or something and you wondered what had happened. What had happened was that Daddy had snipped the bedroom scene. He came from a time when if the couple went into the bedroom all you saw was the wind rustling through window shades.

The theatre closed in 1975, though it has seen several tenants—and uses—since then, including serving as a temporary home for more than one church.

In the mid-1980s, a local group tried to establish a community theatre for plays, concerts and other events in the Sunset. That effort failed for lack of funds, but opening night for the group proved that there was support for revitalizing the theatre.

On that night, the Tommy Dorsey Orchestra played for an audience of more than 350. Some dressed casually and some came attired in evening gowns and tuxedos.

City officials have proceeded slowly with plans for renovation, trying to chart a course for a twenty-first-century facility the community can be proud of while preserving its twentieth-century appeal—pleasing, to the extent possible, the mental image many residents have of the place from days gone by.

Two proposed changes in future renovations have met with the greatest outcry: changing the marquee, and moving the entrance from the original theatre building to the building beside it.

What many people do not realize, or perhaps remember, is that the theatre has had several different marquees in its day, not just one from the 1950s era that was removed after the city bought the building. That marquee was in poor condition, and its removal revealed decorative touches on the façade that had been obscured for decades.

Moving the front door is not an option. The current entrance does not meet the federal mandate for handicap accessibility.

A number of cosmetic upgrades on the theatre—new paint, new carpet, new curtains on the stage—have prompted some to complement city officials on the good job of renovation.

But the real work of transforming the place into "a crown jewel" lies ahead.

Council members gave approval to a marquee design in May 2008, one that combines an old-fashioned look with new-fangled digital technology. They also gave a tentative nod to a floor plan for the first stage of renovation.

But the show must go on.

The Sunset Theatre was booked for close to two hundred events in 2007, many sponsored by the city, including children's movies, classic films and concerts, including a series billed as Friday Night Bluegrass.

THE POTTERY CAPITAL
OF NORTH CAROLINA

Where there's clay, there's fire. That just might serve as a good slogan for the potters of the Seagrove area of Randolph and surrounding counties, known far and wide as the pottery capital of North Carolina.

The men and women who have practiced this craft locally for some two hundred years have shaped clay into pots and plates and all manner of interesting things and fired them in kilns large and small, using wood, electricity and gas.

When a kiln door opens on a load after firing, it's Christmas, whether it's December or July.

The introduction for a booklet published on the occasion of the first Seagrove Pottery Festival in 1982 credits the hardworking and creative practitioners.

> The potters of Piedmont North Carolina hold a unique position in the United States because they have a continual tradition of pottery making, dating back before the American Revolution. In all other areas of the country, the traditions that existed for hundreds of years died out before or during World War II.
>
> Why has this Piedmont tradition of pottery making continued, in some families for as many as eight or nine generations? Perhaps one of the reasons for the continued tradition is the ability of these potters to meet the changing needs of the public.

Potters have been calling Randolph County home for more than two hundred years. *Courtesy of Randolph County Tourism/Albright.*

In 2005, the members of the North Carolina legislature voted to designate the Seagrove area as the state birthplace of North Carolina traditional pottery, validating something most people have known for eons.

The bill states that "the art of crafting pottery in North Carolina began around 1750 in the Seagrove area, which today includes portions of Randolph, Montgomery, Moore and Chatham counties…where the craft has been carried on for 200 years and, in some cases, by people who represent the eighth and ninth generation of potters in their families."

Potter Phil Morgan, who is known for his crystalline glazes and whose shop has stood alongside NC 705 on the edge of Seagrove for more than thirty years, told a reporter for the Asheboro *Courier-Tribune* that there was plenty of recognition to go around.

"For the state to recognize us as the historical pottery community that we are is a great honor. Not only is the Seagrove area the birthplace of pottery—North Carolina is rapidly becoming known as the pottery state."

Denny Mecham, the executive director of the North Carolina Pottery Center in Seagrove, can see that the area is unique, even if area residents cannot. A Virginia native, she brought a fresh perspective to the job when she arrived in 2004. In early 2005, Mecham told writer Mary Anderson with the Asheboro *Courier-Tribune*:

> *People who live here take for granted that potters live and work here because they always have. For over 250 years, in fact. People who come from other parts of North Carolina and other states are astounded at this unique community of artists. There is nothing like it anywhere else—and they have a wonderful opportunity to see artists at work without pretense.*

Mecham sees the good name of Seagrove-area pottery growing because of the approximately one hundred entrepreneurs, small business owners whose business happens to be pots, working very hard at what they do.

The Pottery Center promotes an awareness of the Tar Heel State's pottery heritage through exhibitions (permanent and changing exhibits of historical and contemporary work); education (self-guided tours, demonstrations and workshops); outreach (museum, community and public school partnerships and grant programs); and visitor services (information on both Seagrove-area and statewide pottery communities, maps, directions and resources). The permanent exhibit of the North Carolina Pottery Center traces North Carolina pottery from prehistoric Native Americans to potters of the twenty-first century.

The website for the Museum of North Carolina Traditional Pottery says there are more than ninety potters within a twenty-mile radius, some of them eighth- and ninth-generation artisans.

Among the local traditions is an annual pottery festival, which was held for the twenty-sixth year last fall, sponsored by the Museum of North Carolina Traditional Pottery. The festival is held at Seagrove School.

The Museum of North Carolina Traditional Pottery, for its part, is moving to a new home after decades in town hall. Its digs will grow from 148 square feet to about 4,500 square feet. The nonprofit organization purchased a former grocery store building on Main Street (NC 705), across from a hardware store in the center of town.

The space will be used to display pots made by a variety of Seagrove-area potters. Plans call for a small coffee shop, a tourist information center and gift shop with books and souvenirs—but not pottery. Many of the ninety-plus Seagrove-area potters have displays up and others have reserved shelf space. The museum has long had a display of one piece by every potter and that has moved with it to the new location.

Membership dues, donations, grants and proceeds from the annual festival have funded the museum and its projects, including printing and distributing nearly 100,000 black-and-white maps each year, showing the way to the area potteries, and a pictorial pottery shop booklet that featured pen-and-ink drawings of shop exteriors. In 2005, the museum printed 80,000 copies of a colorful map of the area potteries with photos of their work and launched a website.

The museum sponsors five special events each year to promote and market the area: Winterfest, held the third weekend in February; Summerfest, the third weekend in June; Christmas in July, the third weekend in July; the Seagrove Pottery Festival, the weekend before Thanksgiving each November; and the Christmas Open House, on the first weekend in December.

A 1932 article in the *High Point Enterprise* notes that Prohibition and progress had nearly put a stop to the age-old art of pottery making: "When china ware from 'the five and ten' replaced the old earthen ware of our ancestors for many generations," wrote Harriette Hammer Walker, "and when prohibition some twenty odd years ago removed the need of the pottery jug, the potters' wheel became idle, or practically so in North Carolina."

But things were not as bleak in the 1930s as they had been a few years earlier, when a couple named Jacques and Julian Busbee changed the face of the local pottery industry.

Mrs. Busbee found a bright orange pottery pie plate with green flecks at the Davidson County State Fair in 1915 and fell in love with it. The Raleigh artists traced the plate to Moore County:

> *To the amazement of Mr. Busbee, he found the potters who still operated their shops in this historic Staffordshire section were chiefly men well past middle life who, when they had made milk crocks, flower pots, churns and a few other pieces, turned their hands to farming as a means of support, for the ware then sold for only a few cents per gallon.*

The sons of the men, with generations of craftsmanship in their hands, were straying away to sawmills, factories and any job that would offer a living wage.

The Busbees saw an opportunity to work with the potters and supply wares to a market eager for such "primitive expressions of isolated rural populations."

They founded Jugtown Pottery and hired potters to make pots for them to market. Juliana Busbee opened a tearoom to sell the wares in Greenwich Village, and later uptown New York City. At first, the potters produced the utilitarian pieces they were accustomed to making—platters, pitchers, pickle jars and such.

The Busbees worked with the potters on shape and form and glazes, introducing Oriental themes and the notion of making decorative pieces. They created a shop that brought prosperity and fame to themselves and to the community.

The first potter to work with the Busbees was J.H. Owen, one of those men in "middle life" of which Walker wrote. But the next two potters, Charlie Teague and Ben Owen, were about twenty when they first turned at Jugtown. Mr. Busbee died in 1947; his wife died in 1959. Today, Vernon and Pam Owens own and operate the pottery, which earned a listing on the National Register of Historic Places in 1999.

Not all of Randolph's pottery shops are in the southern section of the county.

A single example is New Salem Pottery, north of Randleman, operated by Hal and Eleanor Pugh since 1984. According to a small article in the official booklet published for the eighth annual Seagrove Pottery Festival, their shop is located on land associated with five potters—J.M. Hayes, George Newby, Thomas and William Dennis and Peter Dicks—who had either owned the land, or worked there, since 1790.

Where there's pottery in Randolph County, there is history.

And there is clay.

And fire.

The North Carolina Pottery Center, at 233 East Avenue in Seagrove, is open Tuesday– Saturday, 10:00 a.m. to 4:00 p.m. As of May 2008, admission is two dollars for adults, one dollar for students ninth through twelfth grades and free for younger students. For information, call 336.873.8430 or send an email to ncpc@atomic.net.

For more information about the Museum of North Carolina Traditional Pottery and its work, call 336.873.7887, send an email to ncpottery122@embarqmail.com or write to P.O. Box 500, Seagrove, North Carolina, 27341. The museum is open Monday through Friday, but the hours vary—call for information. The organization's website (www.seagrovepotteryheritage.com) has information on more than one hundred pottery shops.

THE FIRST STATE ZOO

Lions and tiger rattlesnakes and polar bears. Oh my.

And bullfrogs and bison and gemsbok. And impala and kookaburra and gar. And red wolves and sea lions and scarlet ibis.

Oh my.

And don't forget the plants. Milkweed and saguaro and yellow monkey weed. And inkberry and cattail and beard-tongue. And Venus flytrap and ginseng and sweet pepperbush.

Oh my.

The North Carolina Zoo is a Randolph County gem, a cornucopia of animals and plants.

The zoo is the nation's largest walk-through, natural-habitat zoo. Its Africa and North America "continents" feature five miles of walkways on five hundred acres. Another nine hundred acres are available for development.

But that is not all.

Its stated mission is "to encourage understanding of and commitment to the conservation of the world's wildlife and wild places through the recognition of the interdependence of people and nature. We will do this by creating a sense of enjoyment, wonder and discovery throughout the park and in our outreach programs."

The State of North Carolina pioneered one of the first state symphonies, the first state museum of art and the first state school for the performing arts.

The North Carolina Zoo offers up close and personal glimpses of wild animals—and wild plants, too. *Courtesy of the North Carolina Zoo.*

The Raleigh Jaycees got the ball rolling in 1964, when they hosted a professional football game to raise money to study the idea of establishing the first state zoo. The game generated $18,000.

Three years later, a nine-member commission created by the state legislature—called the North Carolina Zoological Garden Study Commission—reported that building a zoo in the Tar Heel State would not only be feasible, but that it was a project that should be pursued. Legislators established a state zoological authority with a fifteen-member board of directors to find a place to build a zoo.

While twenty-seven communities across the state initially expressed interest in making a bid, in the final analysis just six threw their hats into the ring as potential sites: Albemarle, Asheboro, Butner, Concord, Chatham County and Statesville.

The state had set out strict rules for communities trying to woo the zoo. One of them was that at least one thousand acres of land had to be made available, free and clear of all encumbrances, and at no cost to the state. Another condition was that utilities, including water, sewer, gas and electric service, had to be provided by local government to the border of the park.

D. Wescott Moser, Asheboro's mayor pro tem, chaired a Randolph County Zoological Committee, whose members pursued the opportunity with gusto. David Stedman chaired a fundraising effort to secure moneys needed to purchase property and to provide the required $150,000 pledge to demonstrate, according to state guidelines, "tangible evidence that there exists a local, active organization which is principally concerned with development of this park in its area."

The local committee scoured the Randolph landscape for a suitable site. They picked two for consideration.

One tract included Purgatory Mountain, an area with scenic views and rolling terrain five miles southeast of Asheboro. The second site was near the community of Ulah, seven miles southwest of Asheboro, a tract recommended by accessibility and a sizable stream.

The Randolph County zoo supporters did their homework well.

After two months of touring and intense inspections of each site, site-selection committee members recommended to the authority board of directors that Asheboro should host the zoo. Concord was suggested as an alternate site. On February 20, 1971, board members approved the recommendation of Asheboro. The North Carolina Zoological Society, a nonprofit organization, was established to raise money for the zoo.

The Randolph County Society for Zoological Development gave 1,371 acres of land—the Purgatory Mountain site—to the zoo society in October 1971. The first park ranger was hired in February 1972; at a dedication ceremony a month later, North Carolina Governor Bob Scott declared the zoo site a primitive recreation area for daytime use by the public. Voters approved a $2 million zoo bond referendum in May 1972.

The first zoo director, William Hoff of the St. Louis Zoo, was hired in February 1973. The zoo's first animals, a pair of Galapagos tortoises, arrived in June 1973. They were purchased by the zoo society at a cost of $5,000. In late 1973, zoological authority members approved a master plan concept prepared by J. Hyatt Hammond and Associates of Asheboro and Greensboro.

Construction started on what was known as the "Interim Zoo," an area where animals would be held until natural habitat environments could be built.

In August 1974, the first animal born at the zoo, a slow loris, arrived.

By the fall of 1975, the Interim Zoo covered forty acres; the animal collection included more than 155 mammals, reptiles and birds of 55 species.

The grand opening of Africa, the first zoo "continent," was held on June 28, 1980. Governor Jim Hunt dedicated five new habitats—for elephant, rhinoceros, lion, chimpanzee and baboon.

An early zoo brochure explained to visitors that the North Carolina Zoological Park was different:

> *You're about to begin a trip through a zoo which is probably unlike any other zoo you have ever visited. This is a natural habitat zoo. Don't look for traditional enclosures. Instead, watch for ostriches strutting past a herd of zebras near giraffes stretching to nibble tree leaves.*
>
> *Stroll past baboons cavorting on their rocky island. Ride a tram through acres of grassy banks, streams and boulders where African animals roam, stomp and frolic as they do in the wild. It's a world where elephants trumpet and lions crouch.*

In 1993, Dr. David Jones, a former director of the London Zoo, was named the zoo's third director. Jones replaced Robert Fry, who had held the job since 1978.

Family Life magazine named the zoo one of the top five in the nation in 1994, the same year that the North America "continent" opened.

The zoo's annual attendance reached its highest mark in a decade for the fiscal year ending June 30, 2007, with 746,650. The mark ranks as the fourth highest annual attendance mark in the zoo's thirty-three-year history. The single-year record of 934,455 was set during fiscal year 1994–95 and was largely due to the grand opening of North America, with a large number of new exhibits.

The flocks of zoo visitors placed the park in third place on the list of most visited attractions among North Carolina's public and private museum and historic sites. The top two destinations in the category were Asheville's Biltmore House and Charlotte's Discovery Place.

"Many residents, especially those who have arrived in North Carolina in the last few years," said Jones, "don't know just what a unique and magical place we have."

In the mid-1990s, Jones led a shift in the direction of the zoo, moving away from the master plan concept to build seven continents, showcasing animals representative of each continent. That idea, according to Jones, would take too much time and too much money.

A zoo should be a showcase for animals, Jones said, but also for plants, water, conservation efforts and exhibits that show how animals and humans are interdependent.

The zoo's vision, summed up:

> *We will be the most attractive and relevant place on the eastern side of the United States connecting people with their natural environment. Our living collections, exhibits and programs, including the Earth Resources Center, and all our outreach activities will present conservation and environmental stewardship in the most interesting, meaningful, and entertaining way. While the park will always be the headquarters and focus of much of our activity, our outreach programs will extend to all citizens of North Carolina and will have an impact on people's thinking and actions both locally and globally.*

The North Carolina Zoo, south of Asheboro, is open 364 days a year—April 1 through October 31 from 9:00 a.m. to 5:00 p.m. and November 1 through March 31 from 9:00 a.m. to 4:00 p.m. The park is closed on Christmas Day and during severe weather. For information, call 1.800.488.0444.

THE "PLANE" TRUTH—THIS MUSEUM HAS WINGS

Jim Peddycord's dream has taken flight. Today, it is called the North Carolina Aviation Museum and it is the future home of the North Carolina Aviation Hall of Fame.

The museum has seventeen authentically restored, airworthy aircraft on display. It also houses a large collection of military uniforms, medals, memorabilia and other historic artifacts from World War II through the Vietnam War; while the focus is on military aviation, there are displays about civilian aviation, too, including a corner devoted to Piedmont Airlines. The museum store has the largest collection of model airplanes in the South.

It is a place where one can sit and listen as pilots recount adventures from days gone by, or watch an airplane engine (or maybe an entire plane) being rebuilt. The nonprofit facility sometimes brings tears to the eyes of old-timers and sometimes puts smiles on the faces of young people.

Peddycord was an Asheboro businessman who loved flying and was interested in collecting old military aircraft. So, in 1996, he founded the Foundation for Aircraft Conservation, a museum with three warbirds at the Asheboro airport, and put together an air show.

Just three days before the second air show, in the summer of 1997, Peddycord and his son Rick were killed when their small planes collided and crashed in the Randolph County countryside near the community of Coleridge.

Other aviation enthusiasts, including another Asheboro businessman named Craig Branson, kept the fledgling operation airborne. They changed the name to the Peddycord Foundation for Aircraft Preservation.

The museum, one of three aviation museums in the state, began in a single hangar. Soon that building was brimming with aircraft and a wide-ranging collection of wartime memorabilia. A second hangar was completed in 2001. At first, the sole occupant of the second hangar was a Mitchell B-25, dubbed "Carolina Girl."

Volunteers worked on the restoration of the twin-engine bomber until 2004; the plane, which was on long-term loan, rotated out of the museum inventory two years later.

State legislators approved the facility's designation as the North Carolina Aviation Museum in 2003, at the same time recognizing the site as the future home of the North Carolina Aviation Hall of Fame. In 2008, there was still no money to build a home for the Hall of Fame.

"I think it's a very worthwhile project given our history," said Ben Marion, a former general manager of the museum who sits on the board. "North Carolina was very much in the forefront of aviation history from its development on. There'll be no shortage of people who can be in this. It needs to be done."

Prime candidates for induction right off the bat, Marion said, are the Wright Brothers, who flew their heavier-than-air machine at Kitty Hawk,

Most of the aircraft in the collection at the North Carolina Aviation Museum are airworthy. *Courtesy Randolph County Tourism/Schoenberger.*

North Carolina, on December 17, 1903; World War II flying ace George Preddy Jr. of Greensboro; and Zeke Saunders, a longtime official with North Carolina's Piedmont Airlines, a regional airline that operated out of Winston-Salem.

The Hall of Fame will not just be for North Carolina natives or residents, Marion said, but also for nonnatives and nonresidents affiliated with milestone aviation events that occurred in the Old North State.

Roy Gilliland, a military historian who assumed duties as curator and general manager in 2006, described the North Carolina Aviation Museum as unique:

> *Few museums have aircraft that could be flown at a moment's notice. There are two schools of thought on historic aircraft. Our viewpoint is these aircraft were made to fly. They were made to be used. We want to have a living-type museum. The other philosophy is they are very historic in nature and you should never fly them because something could happen to them.*

The museum owns six planes, but since the rest of the aircraft are on loan, the collection changes. Among the aircraft on display in June of 2008 were: a Piper J-3 Flitfire that was flown by Orville Wright in 1943; a Stearman, one of the most widely used training aircraft for the military in the 1940s; and a Cessna L-19, nicknamed "Bird Dog" because the aircraft's mission was simple—to seek out enemy positions, order air strikes and assess the damage, usually while flying at tree level.

The newest additions: a Shehane Aerosport *Quail* and a Purcell *Flightsail Pelican* experimental flying boat (the only one in the world); a U.S. Coast Guard/United States Department of Homeland Security *Condor* unmanned aerial reconnaissance vehicle; a Burt Rutan-designed VariEze aircraft built of composite materials, which will be fully restored; and a rare Fairchild Aircraft Company F-22, a two-place single-wing civilian airplane built in 1934 during the "golden age" of aviation.

The museum has members from all over the country, and some from other countries. Some members fly in every few months; some show up nearly every day the museum is open. Most are aviation buffs, but not all. Some ten thousand people visit the museum each year.

"Some people are just like me," Gilliland said. "Maybe they could land a plane in an emergency, but don't know an aileron from whatever."

People learn about the museum and donate everything from books (a retired lieutenant colonel donated more than two hundred) and photographs to uniforms and flight instruments—any air- or military-related paraphernalia. All donations are welcomed.

"Unless places like this perpetuate the memories and keep it going and remember the sacrifices of men and women, unless the memory is kept alive," Gilliland said, "it's going to be a cultural crisis because people are going to forget…This is an important mission to me—perpetuating the public education."

A Walk of Fame sidewalk leading to the museum is paved with bricks engraved with names. The project is a fundraiser. For a tax-deductible gift of one hundred dollars, a donor can have his or her name etched into a brick, or the name of a family member or special friend, or even a company name.

The museum is located at Asheboro Regional Airport, off of NC 49 on Pilots View Road, about five miles south of Asheboro. For information about the North Carolina Aviation Museum, visit www.ncairmuseum.org or call 336.625.0170.

WANT A HARLEY
WITH THAT HAMBURGER?

Ed Rich shares a joke with customers who bring their motorcycles to his shop for work.

He takes test spins after repairs are done and, when the owner comes to pick up the bike, Rich breaks the news that something is wrong with the steering.

"What's wrong with it?" a customer will ask.

"I headed out the other day," Rich will reply, trying not to grin, "and like to never got it to turn around."

Well, truth be known, Rich is probably not joking.

He'd prefer to be out on the road on their Harley, or his Harley, or *somebody's* Harley.

But he's usually too busy working.

He runs the American Classic Motorcycle Company in a two-story building on U.S. 64 West in the Randolph County seat of Asheboro. The building houses a shop, a diner and a museum.

The full-service shop specializes in the restoration and repair of Harley-Davidson motorcycles produced between 1936 and 1984 and sells parts, clothing and used motorcycles. Rich also teaches a course on antique motorcycle restoration for Randolph Community College in the shop. The series of courses is designed to teach a student to restore a complete motorcycle.

The Heritage Diner serves breakfast and lunch under bike-related menu headings such as fly wheels (those are waffles), saddle bags (side orders, if you please) and low rides (salads).

One of the largest collections of privately owned Harley-Davidson motorcycles is in Asheboro. *Courtesy of Paul Church.*

The second floor is a museum, housing one of the largest collections of privately owned Harleys in the world. A register shows that visitors have come from all fifty states, and from some twenty-five other countries. Admission is free.

Among the machines a visitor to this mini-Mecca for motorcycle enthusiasts will find are a 1936 H-D Knucklehead, a 1938 Knucklehead and a 1940 Knucklehead; a 1948 Panhead and a 1950 Panhead (fiftieth anniversary edition); a 1966 Shovelhead; a 1971 FLH Dresser (All-American edition); and a 1978 MX250 Motocross.

A fully restored 1947 Knucklehead has quite a local history.

It belonged to a fellow named Vernon Moore, who delivered telegrams around Randolph County for more than forty years out of the Western Union office in Asheboro.

The distinctive rumble of Moore's Harley was not a welcomed sound during World War II, when most of his trips were to bring sad news to a family about a soldier or a sailor.

Shortly before his retirement in 1967, Moore recalled those days in a newspaper interview: "There wasn't a hog path in the county I didn't go down delivering telegrams during the war," he said. "Most of them were about a son or a father being missing or killed in action…my busiest time was during the Battle of the Bulge."

He went beyond the call of duty during those difficult assignments, offering a shoulder to cry on or a willing ear for their memories. He often stayed an hour or more before he felt he could leave a grief-stricken family. Eventually, Moore learned to ask a neighbor to meet him at a home where he would be bringing bad news.

The last motorcycle Moore used—he wore out several over the years— wound up in the hands of a man in Florida who had planned to restore it. Ed Rich tracked it down there and found the bike in pieces. The man had taken it apart but never worked on it. After Rich finished talking about the importance of that particular Knucklehead in the history of a small Piedmont North Carolina town, the man sold the bike to him.

Rich brought it back to his shop, where he and his students in the restoration class spent eight months working on the machine. The bike is now displayed in the museum.

Rich is an artist who has painted pictures of old mills and country stores and more reflective works, like the recent canvas portraying an anguished old man seated on a bench, a hand covering his face. He sees a meticulously restored bike as beautiful art.

Preserving an old machine is also important, Rich said, because they are disappearing. He feels fortunate to have saved Moore's bike before it disappeared forever, a box of metal parts discarded on a scrap heap. To Rich, the fact that the bike has a local story makes it worth more.

It is art. And it is history.

Such descriptions can be applied to the museum as a whole. There are vintage advertising, classic magazines and a mélange of motorcycle memorabilia. One section is dedicated to the recreation of a motorcycle dealership, circa 1949. Looking though the glass at the empty shop, a visitor almost expects to see someone walk into the display from a lunch break and return to work.

Rich plans to expand the 3,200-square-foot museum. He has room. He just needs to find the time, since he does the work himself. He also plans to recreate a motorcycle dealership that was established in the Tennessee town of Greenville in 1937. When it closed many years later, it was left as it had been for years. Rich bought the shop, lock, stock and barrel.

The Randolph County motorcycle museum was just one of five Harley-Davidson museums invited to participate in the grand opening of the new company-owned Harley-Davidson Museum in Milwaukee in the summer of 2008.

"I have nothing to do with Harley," Rich said. "I just like their history and the people in their history. The mystique is still there. It hasn't gone away."

The American Classic Motorcycle Museum is open Monday through Saturday. For more information, call 336.629.9564, send an email to acmc@asheboro.com or visit www. american-classic-motorcycle.com.

KIDS, COME TO CAMP AND
START YOUR ENGINES

The miracle of Victory Junction Gang Camp is not measured in the size and scope or even the sheer magic of the NASCAR-themed getaway near Randleman in Randolph County that boasts—among other buildings ringing an asphalt oval—a racecar that is bigger than a house.

No, the measure by which to gauge Victory Junction is found in the smiles, the laughter and the squeals of unabashed delight from children fishing, boating, swimming, playing basketball, riding horses and participating in a host of other activities when camp is in session.

That's because Victory Junction Gang Camp is for children with chronic medical conditions or serious illnesses—children who might not otherwise get a chance to go to a regular camp and do some of the things that regular kids take for granted.

Victory Junction is not just a marvelous destination to sick children and their families. It is a miracle.

The camp is a member of the Association of Hole in the Wall Camps started by actor Paul Newman. The racing Pettys of Randolph County were inspired to build a camp in North Carolina after participating in a motorcycle ride to Camp Boggy Creek in Florida in 1999. Boggy Creek, a year-round camp for seriously ill children, is also a Hole in the Wall camp.

Before any serious plans were made, however, tragedy struck the Pettys—Adam Petty, grandson of the King, Richard Petty, was killed when his car hit the wall in turn three during practice for a Busch race at New Hampshire International Speedway.

Adam's mother, Pattie Petty, told an audience at the Mayor's Prayer Breakfast in Asheboro in 2006 that she, her husband Kyle and the rest of the family struggled with the sudden loss of the charismatic nineteen-year-old. Eventually, she said, they had to face a few questions.

"Do we become powerful or pitiful?"

"Do you let your test be your test or your testimony?"

"What would Jesus do?"

"What would Adam do?"

The family's answer was to tackle building Victory Junction Gang Camp on seventy-two acres donated by Adam's grandparents, Richard and Lynda Petty, like they'd always tackled racing—with their mind, body, heart and soul set on getting to the finish line.

Some people, she said, told them it could not be done.

Some people, of course, were wrong.

Victory Junction welcomed its first campers in June 2004, offering a camping experience for children ages seven through fifteen that is built around a racing theme, with the sights, sounds, look and feel of a racetrack.

The centerpiece has to be a building that was designed and painted to look like Adam Petty's No. 45. Inside campers can "suit up" to change a tire, build and race a miniature wooden car or just get close to a real race car.

There's a "Catch, Kiss & Release Marina" with canoes, kayaks, paddleboats and universally accessible pontoon boats, where every camper can get out on the seven-acre lake, or stay on shore under a covered dock, and try their luck at catching a bass, striper or trout.

There's a water park with a giant motorcycle in the middle of the pool; a climbing tower that can be conquered even by youngsters who spend most of their time in a wheelchair; a barn where campers can see a llama, pet a newborn donkey or ride a pony; a full-size gym; an arts center; a theatre; a treehouse; a maze; a bowling alley; and a miniature golf course.

The children served at Victory Junction may have any of the following health issues: arthritis, asthma, cancer, epilepsy, hemophilia, immunology deficiencies/HIV, sickle cell disease, spina bifida, gastrointestinal disease, heart disease, kidney disease, liver disease, neurological disease, skin disease, cystic fibrosis, transverse myelitis, diabetes, autism, craniofacial anomalies, physical disabilities or may be burn survivors or kids on vents.

Most campers come from North or South Carolina, but about 15 percent travel from elsewhere across the nation. During the summer, more than one thousand children attend weeklong disease-specific camp sessions; the rest of the year, family weekends are offered.

It costs $2,500 for a child to be at the camp for a week, but campers and their families pay nothing. Donations from corporations, organizations and individuals foot the bill. Many of the race teams, owners, drivers and track owners support the camp with individual contributions. Volunteers, including doctors, nurses and other members of the medical staff, help keep the wheels turning, too.

"We have the best medical camp in the United States," said Pattie Petty. "We see more chronically ill children from more disease groups than any other camp in the world. We said we wanted to build a camp where healthy children wished they could come—and I think we have."

Even President George W. Bush seems to agree.

He fit a visit to the camp into a whirlwind trip into Piedmont North Carolina in October 2006. He called Victory Junction a remarkable place and said that he wished more citizens could see the layout. Visitors are not allowed past the front gate during camp sessions.

"The Pettys have been known for a long time as great athletes," Bush said. "Now, they are known as great humanitarians. By building this camp to honor Adam, they have turned a tragic event into a loving event."

As if per the president's wish, more "citizens" will have the opportunity to see Victory Junction, even when camp is in session. In May 2008, work was under way to install a brick pathway leading from the camp entrance to a renovated caboose on the hill. Inside the caboose will be interactive camp displays, history and other information.

It's a respectful distance, protecting the privacy of campers.

Visitors will be able to see what a "remarkable place" Victory Junction is from a visual viewpoint, but, from that distance, they will not be able to see the most impressive feature of the place: those smiles on campers' faces.

But, no doubt, the smiles will be there.

Occasionally, the camp hosts special open house days for past, future and prospective campers, their families and other guests. During one of those bashes, when there were children dancing, swaying, clapping,

Visitors do not get past the front gate when camp is in session at Victory Junction. It's just for kids. *Courtesy of Paul Church.*

playing, eating and laughing in every direction, Pattie Petty surveyed the scene.

"Every time I see these children smile," she said, "I see a little bit of Adam."

Victory Junction Gang Camp was built and operates thanks to contributions; volunteers are needed for everything from being a cabin counselor to helping in the kitchen or office with maintenance and housekeeping. For more information, call 336.498.9055 or visit the camp's web site at www.victoryjunction.org.

LINBROOK HALL—A "HOUSE FOR GIVING"

Linbrook Hall is larger than the numbers indicate. And the numbers are big.

With sixty rooms and more than thirty-two thousand square feet of living space, the house ranks among the largest private homes in the Southeastern United States.

Some two hundred people worked two years to build the house. Workers used more than two hundred tons of steel and more than six million pounds of concrete in the construction.

Designed in the Early Classical Revival style employed in many antebellum mansions in the South, the house's fourteen fluted columns feature Scamozzi capitals, a style named for the sixteenth-century Italian architect Vincenzo Scamozzi. The columns are thirty-two feet tall and four feet in diameter. Visitors enter via a pair of massive mahogany front doors; each door is four inches thick and weighs eight hundred pounds.

With fifteen-foot-tall ceilings throughout most of its interior, Linbrook Hall stands as high as a typical six-story commercial structure. Its central rotunda rises more than sixty feet from the floor in the entrance hall.

The house, furnished with antiques and art from around the world, commands the top of a hill within view of America's oldest mountain range, the Uwharries, standing sentinel in a clearing amidst 450 wooded acres. On a clear day, the view from the cupola—a little room ringed with windows and a widow's walk at the summit of the house—is thirty miles.

Linbrook Hall dwarfs most other private homes in the Southeastern United States in size and in purpose. *Courtesy of Jerry Steele.*

All of that is impressive, architecturally speaking.

But what makes Linbrook Hall even more inspiring, even "larger" than its statistics, is the reason for which Jerry and Linda Neal conceived, planned and built the magnificent home. It was envisioned as a place where lots of people would come together for special events, learn about good causes and, perhaps, be moved to open their pocketbooks—in short, a house for giving.

Jerry Neal is a founder of RF Micro Devices in Greensboro, a company that manufactures critical components that enable wireless devices to transmit and receive signals; half of the cell phones made in the world contain power amplifiers made by RF Micro Devices.

His story is told in a book called *Fire in the Belly: Building a World-leading High-tech Company from Scratch in Tumultuous Times* that was written with Randolph County author Jerry Bledsoe. He and Bledsoe also collaborated on another book, *Built on a Rock: A Memoir of Family, Faith and Place.*

The memoir tells of Neal's roots in Randolph County, the ups and downs of his life and career before RF Micro Devices and, finally, the conception and construction of Linbrook Hall in the rural Randolph community where Neal's family had lived for generations. His grandmother attended nearby Poplar Ridge Friends Meeting, where he learned Quaker values. He remembers long walks with his great-grandfather during which the old farmer passed on a love for place and for the land on which he lived and worked.

Neal said a reader of the book about his business might get the idea that his entrepreneurial life has been easy. The memoir, he said, tells the rest of the story—that everything does not always work the first time. "Sometimes persistence works—and timing." But Neal said he wanted to say more than that—that faith and values can help pave the way for life's successes and sustain one through life's failures.

Another important notion, Neal said, was that those who sometimes just make ends meet, as well as those who make fortunes, can share their blessings. "It's the message of utilizing your good fortune to help make the world a better place, even if it's in a small way."

The Neals are major supporters of a pair of good causes—St. Jude Children's Research Hospital, the world-famous pediatric treatment and research facility founded by Danny Thomas in Memphis, and the Victory Junction Gang Camp, a NASCAR-themed retreat founded by Kyle and Pattie Petty in Randolph County for children with chronic medical conditions or serious illnesses.

"We had a strong desire to help out and to be involved with causes that would further the funding and research for the care of chronically sick children," Neal said. "I had learned that in the South, large homes were used as tools. It wasn't a place to live. It was a place to get business done and to influence other people. And I began to think about the house as a tool."

The house, which was named in honor of his wife, Linda Stewart Neal, and a little brook that winds in front of it, was finished in 2004. As of late spring 2008, Jerry Neal had spent eight nights there. He and his wife are comfortable living in a two-story farmhouse nearby.

"At some point, it is possible that we will live in it," he said. "It's a very low priority. A home like Linbrook Hall, in our opinion, is not a place that's just built to live in. No one needs a place like that to live in."

Tucked away in an upstairs room of the house is a small museum that devotes a section to drawings and pictures of Linbrook Hall in its various stages of construction. There are also sections devoted to the Neals' favorite charities, and one for honors that he has received.

The museum also contains artifacts from his path to business and financial success: a replica of a telephone Neal built when he was a boy; a device that combined a Band-Aid box, a pencil lead, a razor blade and a dry cell battery; a portable radio like his first six-transistor Motorola; and a collection of early cell phones—large, unwieldy devices—the horse-and-buggy versions of today's sleek palm-sized phones.

There is family history here, too, including references to President Herbert Hoover. Jerry Neal and the thirty-first president share a common ancestor—a man named Andreas Huber, who walked with his family from Pennsylvania to Maryland and then, about 1763, to the Uwharrie River, with a wife and twelve children. Huber established a gristmill about a mile from the site of Linbrook Hall after his arrival.

There is the homage to Neal's father, Albert, and his World War II service days, as well as drawings for a 1952 patent the elder Neal received for a woodworking machine, a machine still in production in 2008.

Behind Linbrook Hall, on the edge of a garden, stands a monument—a large rock turned on end, on a rock base. It bears a bronze plaque, with a molded image of Jerry Neal's parents, Albert and Bertie, gazing into each other's eyes. The likenesses were captured from a photograph taken when they were nineteen years old.

Three months before he died in 2001, Albert Neal wrote the words that are inscribed on the plaque:

Built on a Rock

In 1934, this stone lay beside a muddy road, affording a platform for two fourteen-year-olds to get out of the mud and talk. While getting to know each other, a romance developed that lasted a lifetime. Three wonderful children were born into this union—Betty, Jerry and Diane. Now there are grandchildren and great-grandchildren, and still hoping for more, praying they will be God-fearing members of this great nation. All beginning on this solid rock. The fourteen-year-olds were Albert Neal and Bertie Dorsett.

The rock once lay beside a muddy Randolph County country road. Albert and Bertie often met at that rock. Decades after those rendezvous, Albert Neal stopped to ask what had ever happened to the rock that stood near the house he'd lived in as a teen. The man who lived in the house said the rock had been moved years earlier to cover an old well that had gone dry. He showed Albert where it was. A few hours later, the man died.

That spur-of-the-moment inquiry by Albert Neal made it possible for Jerry Neal to rescue that rock years later and give it a place of prominence at Linbrook Hall, a tribute to his parents. Neal said he was grown before he realized that every child did not have loving parents who imparted bedrock values.

The rock stands in perfect alignment with the front and back entrances to Linbrook Hall and to a marble medallion in the floor of the rotunda that marks the center of the house. The placement would have pleased his father, a man who appreciated symmetry, Neal said.

The house and grounds are evolving. Jerry Neal said he and his wife will keep working on the house, probably for as long as they live. In a house of this size, Neal said, there is always something that needs attention. He spends hours most weekends pushing a cart around the mansion, changing light bulbs. He estimates that there are hundreds, perhaps thousands.

Originally, fuel oil was burned to heat water piped underground to heat the house. On a cold winter's day, the boilers consumed one hundred gallons of oil. Now, high-efficiency boilers that burn wood heat the water. It takes a ton of wood to heat the house for a single day, Neal said.

Last year, we burned three gallons of oil the entire year. Those three gallons were used to test the oil boilers to see if they were working. We heated the entire place with scrap wood. My cousin has a sawmill and we're burning scrap wood that would normally be thrown away. Trees blow down on the property—we cut them up and burn them. You couldn't even begin to burn even half of the scrap wood that just falls every year.

One day there may be a formal garden, and maybe a swimming pool. Outdoor amenities now include a skeet-shooting range and ten miles of nature trails that lead to the Uwharrie River. More than two hundred acres of the property are under the forestry management of Dr. Carlyle Franklin, a professor emeritus of North Carolina State University in Raleigh.

"The natural beauty of the property was just outstanding," Neal said, "and it should improve with him managing the forest. Open space is going to be more and more difficult to find. Eventually, we'll hope that people will be able to come enjoy those trails. We're doing a lot of different things. It's all part of the overall attraction with the house being the focal point."

Neal plans to restore his grandparents' farm the way it was in the 1930s and 1940s, part of a rural life historical exhibit that will include the Neals' nearby tractor museum devoted to John Deere machines.

Eventually, Neal said he and his wife would like to give the house to charity.

For now, Linbrook Hall's doors are opened for charity events, but not to the general public.

"We've thought about that," Neal said, "and I think eventually that will be something that will evolve because so many people, when they come to the charity events, they say, 'I wish my aunt, or my brother, or my sister, could see this. Is there any way?'"

"It probably would be logical," he said. "One of the values of a place like this is to have it open to people for people to be able to enjoy it. And, if a charity owned it, it would be a logical way to defer expenses. It would be nice to share it with more people."

The first fundraising event held at Linbrook Hall, a concert with rhythm and blues legend Percy Sledge, brought in $50,000 for the Victory Junction Gang Camp. Another event in association with Kathryn Crosby, the widow of the late Bing Crosby, generated money for the blind. A gathering to raise money for St. Jude Children's Hospital is planned for fall of 2008. The featured entertainer is scheduled to be country singer and fiddler Charlie Daniels, another major supporter of the research hospital.

Randolph County writer Jerry Bledsoe characterizes Linbrook Hall, and its purpose, as one of the most significant things ever to touch Randolph County.

"It's just an incredible thing to have here in Randolph County," he said. "Really great things are going to happen in this house. It's going to bring great things to Randolph County."